CW00361917

The
Grand
Prix
Almanac

Jason Woolgar

Eric Dobby Publishing

Published by Eric Dobby Publishing Ltd,
12 Warnford Road, Orpington, Kent BR6 6LW

A catalogue record of this book is available from the
British Library.

ISBN 1-85882-030-8

Title page photograph:
Michael Schumacher,
winner of the 1994
Formula One World Championship

Typeset in Times by Kevin O'Connor, Poole
Printed and bound in Great Britain by
BPC Hazell Books Ltd
A member of
The British Printing Company Ltd

**This book is dedicated to
the memory of
Ayrton Senna
and
Roland Ratzenberger**

Acknowledgements

A book of this kind takes a great deal of research and I am most grateful for the assistance I have received from the following:

Each of the fourteen 1994 manufactures, who fully co-operated with this publication. Particularly to Ann Bradshaw at Williams, Louise Goodman at Jordan and Eddie Jordan himself for kindly providing the Foreword.

Express Newspapers for the photograph of Riccardo Patrese and ZOOOM Photographic Ltd for the photographs of Thierry Boutsen, Vannick Dalmas and Nicola Larini.

Also to the officials at the following Grand Prix circuits: Adelaide, Barcelona, Hockenheim, Monza and Suzuka.

I am also indebted to Trevor R. Griffiths who allowed me to use details from his book *Grand Prix* and Derek Wright, Editor of *F1 News* who provided detailed race results from his magazine.

Finally I would like to say a special thank you to Kim Sykes who painstakingly checked every page.

Contents

*1994 World Champion Michael Schumacher after the
San Marino Grand Prix*

Foreword
by Eddie Jordan

1994 was a memorable year, both for Jordan Grand Prix and
for Formula One as a whole.

Looking at it first from a personal point of view, our team
made some important steps forward last year. Rubens
Barrichello brought his car home in third place at the second
race of the season, the Pacific Grand Prix, to record our first
ever rostrum finish. He went on to achieve both his and the
team's first ever pole position after a magnificent qualifying
performance in the wet at the Belgian event. Eddie Irvine had
a slightly more troubled start to his racing season, but he
worked hard, consistently qualifying in the top ten, and
towards the end of the year the points began to come his way
too.

We finished 1994 fifth in the Constructors' series, equalling
our best-ever World Championship position. With a works-
engine from Peugeot for 1995, and the continued services of
two of the sport's brightest young talents, Rubens Barrichello
and Eddie Irvine, our future is looking brighter than ever.

My joy at our progress in 1994 was however tinged with
sadness at the tragedies which befell our sport last year. The
death of F1 newcomer Roland Ratzenberger, in practice for
the San Marino Grand Prix, sent shockwaves throughout our
community. The death the following day of three times
World Champion Ayrton Senna sent shockwaves throughout
the world. It was the blackest of weekends for Formula One.
Various regulation changes in the wake of San Marino and
additional well-documented controversies contributed to an
unsettled period mid-season, but by the end of the year the
racing was back to the fore. *The Grand Prix Almanac*
provides a thorough review of the Championship battle and I
am pleased to be associated with a publication which
examines such an eventful Grand Prix year in such detail. It
contains the full results of every race as well as informative
profiles of each driver, manufacturer and circuit. The
records' section is equally extensive, featuring every major
Grand Prix record since the inaugural World Championship
in 1950.

Our sport has changed dramatically since then and the 1995
season heralds the implementation of further changes which
have been designed not only to make the racing safer, but,
hopefully, to increase its entertainment value for the millions
of Grand Prix fans around the world. It's the start of a new
era for Formula One - and a new era for Jordan Grand Prix as

we gear ourselves up for our most emphatic assault to date on the World Championship.

This book provides all the essential information that any motor-racing enthusiast will need in 1995. It should be an ideal companion to what we hope will be an excellent season, particularly for Total Jordan Peugeot!

Eddie Jordan

The new 1995 Jordan Peugeot

Introduction

Despite the closest and most exciting World Championship climax for years, 1994 was by no means a vintage season for Formula 1.

The Grand Prix world had already been rocked by the death of the popular young Austrian driver Roland Ratzenberger when Imola witnessed the last chapter in Ayrton Senna's titanic career. As if the death of one of the greatest drivers was not enough, the sport further suffered a catalogue of accidents and controversy devaluing the remaining races. Rumours continually surfaced that some teams were competing with illegal drivers' aids, and numerous rule changes implemented by the FIA, although helping to allay fears over safety, did little to silence the critics.

There were several other lamentable incidents. The Benetton team were twice implicated in episodes that saw their driver and convincing Championship leader, Michael Schumacher, disqualified. The 16 points that Schumacher lost for these two disqualifications and his subsequent two-race ban saw the ever impressive Damon Hill close the German's once seemingly insurmountable lead to just one point prior to the final race at Adelaide. There, Schumacher, pushed to the limit to defend his lead from the charging Hill, and driving a car damaged in a heavy crash moments earlier, swerved into the Williams' driver ending his Championship dreams.

It was obvious that Schumacher had taken the view that Hill would not pass at any cost, and even with a badly damaged car would not relinquish his lead. It was a fitting end to a controversial and acrimonious Championship.

If a World Championship can be decided in one race there was clearly no doubt that Damon Hill deserved to win it at Adelaide. He drove the race of his short but illustrious career and would undoubtedly have gone on to win if Schumacher had not closed the door so irrevocably on him.

However one race does not a champion make and there can be little doubt that, in the absence of Senna, Michael Schumacher was the outstanding driver of 1994 and certainly deserved to become the first ever German to take the title. For the majority of the season he was a class above the rest. Not including his two disqualifications he finished first in 9 of 14 races and second in three more. If it were not for the penalties incurred by his Benetton team he would have, in all probability, won the Championship by round twelve.

Although Damon Hill would have felt cheated in Australia, Schumacher certainly would have been, if the 16 points deducted and the 20 points Hill had accrued in his absence had seen the title evade him.

Michael Schumacher in the lead of the Australian Grand Prix, 1994

For Damon Hill, Adelaide was a bitter blow. He had worked incredibly hard all season to reduce Schumacher's commanding lead. It was a brave and stunning effort particularly in light of the tragedy that befell his team-mate. He came of age as a great driver at Adelaide and it is generally forgotten, so good have his performances been, that 1994 was only his second full season in Formula 1. He has already won an incredible nine races from just 34 starts, a record significantly better than Schumacher's ten wins in 52 races.

Like all things new the 1995 season promises much. The Schumacher/Hill duel will continue with the added bonus of both drivers having equally competitive team-mates in Johnny Herbert and David Coulthard respectively. Jordan, after their engine deal with Peugeot, look well placed to challenge the four major constructors and Nigel Mansell, if McLaren can produce a more competitive car, could well force Frank Williams to bitterly regret his extraordinary decision to sign the talented but inexperienced Scot David Coulthard.

With these many exciting confrontations ahead it can only be hoped that the 1995 season is not marred by the controversy experienced this year. Rumours continue to persist that some teams are still running illegal driver aids and unless the beleaguered FIA begin to act with some authority these doubts will seriously affect the sport's credibility.

More importantly Formula 1 cannot afford the tragedies which befell it last year and whatever your abiding memories of 1994, ultimately we should all remember Roland Ratzenberger and Ayrton Senna.

Jason Woolgar

1994 Results

*Eric Bernard and Olivier Panis on the podium after the
German Grand Prix, 1994 – the surprise result of the season*

FIA FORMULA 1 WORLD CHAMPIONSHIP - ROUND 1

Brazilian Grand Prix
Interlagos - 27/03/94

Pos	Grid	Driver	Team	Race Time	Diff
1	(2)	M. Schumacher	Benetton	1:35'38.759	
2	(4)	D. Hill	Williams	1:36'04.483	1 Lap
3	(3)	J. Alesi	Ferrari	1:36'39.334	1 Lap
4	(14)	R. Barrichello	Jordon	1:36'46.976	1 Lap
5	(10)	U. Katayama	Tyrrell	1:35'49.727	2 Laps
6	(7)	K. Wendlinger	Sauber	1:35'55.372	2 Laps
7	(21)	J. Herbert	Lotus	1:36'17.478	2 Laps
8	(15)	P. Martini	Minardi	1:36'55.657	2 Laps
9	(18)	E. Comas	Larrousse	1:36'44.573	3 Laps
10	(24)	P. Lamy	Lotus	1:36'43.164	3 Laps
11	(19)	O. Panis	Ligier	1:36'44.654	3 Laps
12	(26)	D. Brabham	Simtek	1:36'37.723	4 Laps

Retirements

Pos	Grid	Driver	Team	Lap - Retirement
13	(1)	A. Senna	Williams	Lap 56 - Accident
14	(18)	M. Brundle	McLaren	Lap 35 - Accident
15	(16)	E. Irvine	Jordan	Lap 35 - Accident
16	(9)	J. Verstappen	Benetton	Lap 35 - Accident
17	(20)	E. Bernard	Ligier	Lap 34 - Accident
18	(12)	M. Blundell	Tyrrell	Lap 22 - Accident
19	(11)	C. Fittipaldi	Arrows	Lap 22 - Gearbox
20	(5)	H.H. Frentzen	Sauber	Lap 16 - Accident
21	(8)	M. Hakkinen	McLaren	Lap 14 - Engine
22	(22)	M. Alboreto	Minardi	Lap 8 - Engine
23	(6)	G. Morbidelli	Arrows	Lap 6 - Gearbox
24	(17)	G. Berger	Ferrari	Lap 6 - Hydraulics
25	(23)	O. Beretta	Larrousse	Lap 3 - Accident
26	(25)	B. Gachot	Pacific	Lap 2 - Accident

Non Qualifiers

	Driver	Team	
27	R. Ratzenberger	Simtek	1'22.707
28	P. Belmondo	Pacific	No Time

Fastest Laps
Qualifying: A. Senna - 1'15.962
Race: M. Schumacher - 1'18.455

FIA FORMULA 1 WORLD CHAMPIONSHIP - ROUND 2

Pacific Grand Prix
Aida - 17/04/94

Pos	Grid	Driver	Team	Race Time	Diff
1	(2)	M. Schumacher	Benetton	1:46'01.693	
2	(5)	G. Berger	Ferrari	1:47'16.993	1'15.300
3	(8)	R. Barrichello	Jordan	1:46'17.605	1 Lap
4	(9)	C. Fittipaldi	Arrows	1:46'58.555	1 Lap
5	(11)	H.H. Frentzen	Sauber	1:47'08.922	1 Lap
6	(16)	E. Comas	Larrousse	1:46'04.616	3 Laps
7	(23)	J. Herbert	Lotus	1:47'05.707	3 Laps
8	(24)	P. Lamy	Lotus	1:46'30.007	4 Laps
9	(22)	O. Panis	Ligier	1:46'11.748	5 Laps
10	(18)	E. Bernard	Ligier	1:46'33.385	5 Laps
11	(26)	R. Ratzenberger	Simtek	1:47'01.984	5 Laps

Retirements

Pos	Grid	Driver	Team	Lap-Retirement
12	(13)	G. Morbidelli	Arrows	Lap 70 - Engine
13	(19)	K. Wendlinger	Sauber	Lap 70 - Accident
14	(15)	M. Alboreto	Minardi	Lap 70 - Accident
15	(6)	M. Brundle	McLaren	Lap 68 - Engine
16	(17)	P. Martini	Minardi	Lap 64 - Accident
17	(10)	J. Verstappen	Benetton	Lap 55 - Accident
18	(3)	D. Hill	Williams	Lap 50 - Transmission
19	(20)	A. Suzuki	Jordan	Lap 45 - Steering
20	(14)	U. Katayama	Tyrrell	Lap 43 - Engine
21	(4)	M. Hakkinen	McLaren	Lap 20 - Hydraulics
22	(21)	O. Beretta	Larrousse	Lap 15 - Engine
23	(25)	D. Brabham	Simtek	Lap 3 - Engine
24	(1)	A. Senna	Williams	Lap 1 - Accident
25	(12)	M. Blundell	Tyrrell	Lap 1 - Accident
26	(7)	N. Larini	Ferrari	Lap 1 - Accident

Non Qualifiers

27	B. Gachot	Pacific	1'16.927
28	P. Belmondo	Pacific	1'17.450

Fastest Laps
Qualifying: A. Senna - 1'10.218
Race: M. Schumacher – 1'14.023

FIA FORMULA 1 WORLD CHAMPIONSHIP - ROUND 3

San Marino Grand Prix
Imola - 01/05/94

Pos	Grid	Driver	Team	Race Time	Diff
1	(2)	M. Schumacher	Benetton	1:28'28.642	
2	(6)	N. Larini	Ferrari	1:29'23.584	54.942
3	(8)	M. Hakkinen	McLaren	1:29'39.321	1'10.679
4	(10)	K. Wendlinger	Sauber	1:29'42.300	1'13.658
5	(9)	U. Katayama	Tyrrell	1:28'39.183	1 Lap
6	(4)	D. Hill	Williams	1:28'39.437	1 Lap
7	(7)	H.H. Frentzen	Sauber	1:28'40.518	1 Lap
8	(13)	M. Brundle	McLaren	1:28'54.669	1 Lap
9	(12)	M. Blundell	Tyrrell	1:28'49.109	2 Laps
10	(20)	J. Herbert	Lotus	1:29'02.511	2 Laps
11	(19)	O. Panis	Ligier	1:29'16.475	2 Laps
12	(17)	E. Bernard	Ligier	1:29'43.571	3 Laps

Retirements

Pos	Grid	Driver	Team	Lap-Retirement
13	(16)	C. Fittipaldi	Arrows	Lap 55 - Brakes
14	(21)	A. de Cesaris	Jordan	Lap 50 - Accident
15	(15)	M. Alboreto	Minardi	Lap 45 - Accident
16	(11)	G. Morbidelli	Arrows	Lap 41 - Engine
17	(14)	P. Martini	Minardi	Lap 38 - Accident
18	(24)	D. Brabham	Simtek	Lap 28 - Puncture
19	(25)	B. Gachot	Pacific	Lap 24 - Engine
20	(23)	O. Beretta	Larrousse	Lap 18 - Engine
21	(3)	G. Berger	Ferrari	Lap 17 - Retired
22	(1)	A. Senna	Williams	Lap 6 - Accident
23	(18)	E. Comas	Larrousse	Lap 6 - Accident
24	(5)	J.J. Lehto	Benetton	Lap 1 - Accident
25	(22)	P. Lamy	Lotus	Lap 1 - Accident

Non Starter

26	(26)	R. Ratzenberger	Simtek	Fatal accident

Non Qualifiers

27		P. Belmondo	Pacific	1'27.881
28		R. Barrichello	Jordan	14'57.323 - Accident

Fastest Laps
Qualifying: A. Senna - 1'21.548
Race: D. Hill – 1'24.335

FIA FORMULA 1 WORLD CHAMPIONSHIP - ROUND 4

Monaco Grand Prix
Monaco - 15/05/94

Pos	Grid	Driver	Team	Race Time	Diff
1	(1)	M. Schumacher	Benetton	1:49'55.372	
2	(8)	M. Brundle	McLaren	1:50'32.650	32.278
3	(3)	G. Berger	Ferrari	1:51'12.196	1'16.824
4	(14)	A. de Cesaris	Jordan	1:50'27.791	1 Lap
5	(5)	J. Alesi	Ferrari	1:50'42.460	1 Lap
6	(12)	M. Alboreto	Minardi	1:50'59.689	1 Lap
7	(17)	J.J. Lehto	Benetton	1:51'24.061	1 Lap
8	(18)	O. Beretta	Larrousse	1:50'48.072	2 Laps
9	(20)	O. Panis	Ligier	1:51'12.577	2 Laps
10	(13)	E. Comas	Larrousse	1:50'39.324	3 Laps
11	(19)	P. Lamy	Lotus	1:50'57.586	5 Laps

Retirements

Pos	Grid	Driver	Team	Lap-Retirement
12	(16)	J. Herbert	Lotus	Lap 69 - Gearbox
13	(24)	P. Belmondo	Pacific	Lap 54 - Retired
14	(23)	B. Gachot	Pacific	Lap 50 - Gearbox
15	(6)	C. Fittipaldi	Arrows	Lap 48 - Gearbox
16	(22)	D. Brabham	Simtek	Lap 46 - Accident
17	(10)	M. Blundell	Tyrrell	Lap 41 - Transmission
18	(11)	U. Katayama	Tyrrell	Lap 39 - Gearbox
19	(21)	E. Bernard	Ligier	Lap 35 - Accident
20	(15)	R. Barrichello	Jordan	Lap 28 - Engine
21	(4)	D. Hill	Williams	Lap 1 - Accident
22	(2)	M. Hakkinen	McLaren	Lap 1 - Accident
23	(7)	G. Morbidelli	Arrows	Lap 1 - Accident
24	(9)	P. Martini	Minardi	Lap 1 - Accident

Non Starters
26 K. Wendlinger   Sauber - Accident
27 H.H. Frentzen   Sauber - Withdrawn

Fastest Laps
Qualifying: M. Schumacher - 1'18.560
Race: M. Schumacher - 1'21.078

FIA FORMULA 1 WORLD CHAMPIONSHIP - ROUND 5

Spanish Grand Prix
Barcelona - 29/05/94

Pos	Grid	Driver	Team	Race Time	Diff
1	(2)	D. Hill	Williams	1:36'14.374	
2	(1)	M. Schumacher	Benetton	1:36'38.540	24.166
3	(11)	M. Blundell	Tyrrell	1:37'41.343	1'26.969
4	(6)	J. Alesi	Ferrari	1:36'40.141	1 Lap
5	(18)	P. Martini	Minardi	1:37'12.385	1 Lap
6	(13)	E. Irvine	Jordan	1:37'32.798	1 Lap
7	(19)	O. Panis	Ligier	1:36'44.800	2 Laps
8	(20)	E. Bernard	Ligier	1:36'15.687	3 Laps
9	(23)	A. Zanardi	Lotus	1:37'42.211	3 Laps
10	(24)	D. Brabham	Simtek	1:37'05.051	4 Laps

Retirements

Pos	Grid	Driver	Team	Lap-Retirement
11	(8)	M. Brundle	McLaren	Lap 60 - Transmission
12	(4)	J.J. Lehto	Benetton	Lap 54 - Engine
13	(3)	M. Hakkinen	McLaren	Lap 49 - Engine
14	(22)	J. Herbert	Lotus	Lap 42 - Accident
15	(5)	R. Barrichello	Jordan	Lap 40 - Engine
16	(21)	C. Fittipaldi	Arrows	Lap 36 - Engine
17	(9)	D. Coulthard	Williams	Lap 33 - Electrics
18	(25)	B. Gachot	Pacific	Lap 33 - Accident
19	(7)	G. Berger	Ferrari	Lap 28 - Gearbox
20	(15)	G. Morbidelli	Arrows	Lap 25 - Fuel Line
21	(12)	H.H. Frentzen	Sauber	Lap 22 - Gearbox
22	(16)	E. Comas	Larrousse	Lap 20 - Water Leak
23	(10)	U. Katayama	Tyrrell	Lap 17 - Engine
24	(14)	M. Alboreto	Minardi	Lap 5 - Engine
25	(26)	P. Belmondo	Pacific	Lap 4 - Accident
26	(17)	O. Beretta	Larrousse	Lap 1 - Engine

Non Qualifier

27		A. Montermini	Simtek	1'31.111 - Accident

Fastest Laps
Qualifying: M. Schumacher - 1'21.908
Race: M. Schumacher - 1'25.155

FIA FORMULA 1 WORLD CHAMPIONSHIP - ROUND 6

Canadian Grand Prix
Montreal - 12/06/94

Pos	Grid	Driver	Team	Race Time	Diff
1	(1)	M. Schumacher	Benetton	1:44'31.887	
2	(4)	D. Hill	Williams	1:45'11.547	39.660
3	(2)	J. Alesi	Ferrari	1:45'45.275	1'13.388
4	(3)	G. Berger	Ferrari	1:45'47.496	1'15.609
5	(5)	D. Coulthard	Williams	1:44'32.611	1 Lap
6	(20)	J.J. Lehto	Benetton	1:44'59.463	1 Lap
7	(6)	R. Barrichello	Jordan	1:45'08.017	1 Lap
8	(17)	J. Herbert	Lotus	1:45'48.763	1 Lap
9	(15)	P. Martini	Minardi	1:46'14.702	1 Lap
10	(13)	M. Blundell	Tyrrell	1:43'25.537	2 Laps
11	(18)	M. Alboreto	Minardi	1:45'12.617	2 Laps
12	(19)	O. Panis	Ligier	1:45'13.178	2 Laps
13	(24)	E. Bernard	Ligier	1:45'02.766	3 Laps
14	(25)	D. Brabham	Simtek	1:45'08.928	4 Laps

Retirements

Pos	Grid	Driver	Team	Lap-Retirement
15	(23)	A. Zanardi	Lotus	Lap 63 - Engine
16	(7)	M. Hakkinen	McLaren	Lap 62 - Engine
17	(22)	O. Beretta	Larrousse	Lap 58 - Engine
18	(11)	G. Morbidelli	Arrows	Lap 51 - Engine
19	(26)	B. Gachot	Pacific	Lap 48 - Engine
20	(21)	E. Comas	Larrousse	Lap 46 - Clutch
21	(9)	U. Katayama	Tyrrell	Lap 45 - Accident
22	(8)	E. Irvine	Jordan	Lap 41 - Accident
23	(14)	A. de Cesaris	Sauber	Lap 25 - Engine
24	(10)	H.H. Frentzen	Sauber	Lap 6 - Accident
25	(12)	M. Brundle	McLaren	Lap 4 - Electrics

Disqualified
26 (16) C. Fittipaldi   Arrows   Underweight

Non Qualifier
27 P. Belmondo   Pacific   1'33.006

Fastest Laps
Qualifying: M. Schumacher - 1'26.178
Race: M. Schumacher - 1'28.927

FIA FORMULA 1 WORLD CHAMPIONSHIP - ROUND 7

French Grand Prix
Magny-Cours - 03/07/94

Pos	Grid	Driver	Team	Race Time	Diff
1	(3)	M. Schumacher	Benetton	1:38'35.704	
2	(1)	D. Hill	Williams	1:38'48.346	12.642
3	(5)	G. Berger	Ferrari	1:39'28.469	52.765
4	(10)	H.H. Frentzen	Sauber	1:39'22.743	1 Lap
5	(16)	P. Martini	Minardi	1:38'36.932	2 Laps
6	(11)	A. de Cesaris	Sauber	1:38'44.154	2 Laps
7	(19)	J. Herbert	Lotus	1:38'44.813	2 Laps
8	(18)	C. Fittipaldi	Arrows	1:39'12.438	2 Laps
9	(26)	J. Gounon	Simtek	1:39'02.683	4 Laps
10	(17)	M. Blundell	Tyrrell	1:39'21.944	5 Laps

Retirements

Pos	Grid	Driver	Team	Lap-Retirement
11	(20)	E. Comas	Larrousse	Lap 67 - Engine
12	(14)	U. Katayama	Tyrrell	Lap 54 - Accident
13	(9)	M. Hakkinen	McLaren	Lap 49 - Engine
14	(2)	N. Mansell	Williams	Lap 46 - Transmission
15	(4)	J. Alesi	Ferrari	Lap 42 - Accident
16	(7)	R. Barrichello	Jordan	Lap 42 - Accident
17	(15)	E. Bernard	Ligier	Lap 41 - Gearbox
18	(25)	O. Beretta	Larrousse	Lap 37 - Engine
19	(12)	M. Brundle	McLaren	Lap 30 - Engine
20	(22)	G. Morbidelli	Arrows	Lap 29 - Accident
21	(13)	O. Panis	Ligier	Lap 29 - Accident
22	(24)	D. Brabham	Simtek	Lap 29 - Gearbox
23	(8)	J. Verstappen	Benetton	Lap 26 - Accident
24	(6)	E. Irvine	Jordan	Lap 25 - Gearbox
25	(21)	M. Alboreto	Minardi	Lap 22 - Engine
26	(23)	A. Zanardi	Lotus	Lap 21 - Fire

Non Qualifiers

27	B. Gachot	Pacific	1'21.952
28	P. Belmondo	Pacific	1'23.004

Fastest Laps
Qualifying: D. Hill - 1'16.282
Race: D. Hill - 1'19.678

FIA FORMULA 1 WORLD CHAMPIONSHIP - ROUND 8

British Grand Prix
Silverstone - 10/07/94

Pos	Grid	Driver	Team	Race Time	Diff
1	(1)	D. Hill	Williams	1:30'03.640	
2	(4)	J. Alesi	Ferrari	1:31'11.768	1'08.128
3	(5)	M. Hakkinen	McLaren	1:31'44.299	1'40.659
4	(6)	R. Barrichello	Jordan	1:31'45.391	1'41.751
5	(7)	D. Coulthard	Williams	1:30'06.704	1 Lap
6	(8)	U. Katayama	Tyrrell	1:30'20.793	1 Lap
7	(13)	H.H. Frentzen	Sauber	1:30'23.245	1 Lap
8	(10)	J. Verstappen	Benetton	1:30'45.792	1 Lap
9	(20)	C. Fittipaldi	Arrows	1:30'04.684	2 Laps
10	(14)	P. Martini	Minardi	1:30'20.159	2 Laps
11	(21)	J. Herbert	Lotus	1:30'28.411	2 Laps
12	(15)	O. Panis	Ligier	1:30'38.634	2 Laps
13	(23)	E. Bernard	Ligier	1:30'49.394	2 Laps
14	(24)	O. Beretta	Larrousse	1:30'53.492	2 Laps
15	(25)	D. Brabham	Simtek	1:30'51.590	3 Laps
16	(26)	J. Gounon	Simtek	1:30'52.328	3 Laps

Retirements

Pos	Grid	Driver	Team	Lap-Retirement
17	(17)	M. Alboreto	Minardi	Lap 49 - Engine
18	(3)	G. Berger	Ferrari	Lap 33 - Engine
19	(11)	M. Blundell	Tyrrell	Lap 21 - Gearbox
20	(22)	E. Comas	Larrousse	Lap 13 - Engine
21	(18)	A. de Cesaris	Sauber	Lap 12 - Engine
22	(16)	G. Morbidelli	Arrows	Lap 6 - Fuel Line
23	(19)	A. Zanardi	Lotus	Lap 5 - Engine
24	(9)	M. Brundle	McLaren	Lap 1 - Engine
25	(12)	E. Irvine	Jordan	Lap 1 - Engine

Disqualified
26 (2) M. Schumacher Benetton Black Flag

Non Qualifiers

27 B. Gachot	Pacific	1'31.496
28 P. Belmondo	Pacific	1'32.507

Fastest Laps
Qualifying: D. Hill - 1'24.960
Race: D. Hill - 1'27.100

FIA FORMULA 1 WORLD CHAMPIONSHIP - ROUND 9

German Grand Prix
Hockenheim - 31/07/94

Pos	Grid	Driver	Team	Race Time	Diff
1	(1)	G. Berger	Ferrari	1:22'37.272	
2	(12)	O. Panis	Ligier	1:23'32.051	54.799
3	(14)	E. Bernard	Ligier	1:23'42.314	1'05.042
4	(17)	C. Fittipaldi	Arrows	1:23'58.881	1'21.609
5	(16)	G. Morbidelli	Arrows	1:24'07.816	1'30.544
6	(22)	E. Comas	Larrousse	1:24'22.717	1'45.445
7	(24)	O. Beretta	Larrousse	1:22'44.883	1 Lap
8	(3)	D. Hill	Williams	1:22'47.124	1 Lap

Retirements

Pos	Grid	Driver	Team	Lap-Retirement
9	(26)	J. Gounon	Simtek	Lap 40 - Engine
10	(25)	D. Brabham	Simtek	Lap 38 - Clutch
11	(4)	M. Schumacher	Benetton	Lap 21 - Engine
12	(13)	M. Brundle	McLaren	Lap 20 - Engine
13	(6)	D. Coulthard	Williams	Lap 18 - Gearbox
14	(19)	J. Verstappen	Benetton	Lap 16 - Fire
15	(5)	U. Katayama	Tyrrell	Lap 7 - Throttle
16	(7)	M. Blundell	Tyrrell	Lap 1 - Accident
17	(8)	M. Hakkinen	McLaren	Lap 1 - Accident
18	(21)	A. Zanardi	Lotus	Lap 1 - Accident
19	(15)	J. Herbert	Lotus	Lap 1 - Accident
20	(11)	R. Barrichello	Jordan	Lap 1 - Accident
21	(10)	E. Irvine	Jordan	Lap 1 - Accident
22	(20)	P. Martini	Minardi	Lap 1 - Accident
23	(23)	M. Alboreto	Minardi	Lap 1 - Accident
24	(2)	J. Alesi	Ferrari	Lap 1 - Engine
25	(18)	A. de Cesaris	Sauber	Lap 1 - Accident
26	(9)	H.H. Frentzen	Sauber	Lap 1 - Accident

Non Qualifiers

27	P. Belmondo	Pacific	1'51.122
28	B. Gachot	Pacific	1'51.292

Fastest Laps
Qualifying: G. Berger - 1'43.582
Race: D. Coulthard - 1'46.211

FIA FORMULA 1 WORLD CHAMPIONSHIP - ROUND 10

Hungarian Grand Prix
Hungaroring - 14/08/94

Pos	Grid	Driver	Team	Race Time	Diff
1	(1)	M. Schumacher	Benetton	1:48'00.185	
2	(2)	D. Hill	Williams	1:48'21.012	20.827
3	(12)	J. Verstappen	Benetton	1:49'10.514	1'10.329
4	(6)	M. Brundle	McLaren	1:47'38.809	1 Lap
5	(11)	M. Blundell	Tyrrell	1:48'42.880	1 Lap
6	(9)	O. Panis	Ligier	1:48'43.048	1 Lap
7	(20)	M. Alboreto	Minardi	1:48'07.914	2 Laps
8	(21)	E. Comas	Larrousse	1:48'21.973	2 Laps
9	(25)	O. Beretta	Larrousse	1:48'31.536	2 Laps
10	(18)	E. Bernard	Ligier	1:48'42.793	2 Laps
11	(23)	D. Brabham	Simtek	1:48'27.452	3 Laps
12	(4)	G. Berger	Ferrari	1:42'25.698	5 Laps
13	(22)	A. Zanardi	Lotus	1:48'27.955	5 Laps
14	(16)	C. Fittipaldi	Arrows	1:39'48.866	8 Laps

Retirements

Pos	Grid	Driver	Team	Lap-Retirement
15	(3)	D. Coulthard	Williams	Lap 60 - Accident
16	(13)	J. Alesi	Ferrari	Lap 59 - Gearbox
17	(15)	P. Martini	Minardi	Lap 59 - Accident
18	(8)	H.H. Frentzen	Sauber	Lap 40 - Gearbox
19	(24)	J. Herbert	Lotus	Lap 35 - Electrics
20	(17)	A. de Cesaris	Sauber	Lap 31 - Accident
21	(19)	G. Morbidelli	Arrows	Lap 31 - Accident
22	(14)	P. Alliot	McLaren	Lap 22 - Water Leak
23	(26)	J. Gounon	Simtek	Lap 10 - Handling
24	(5)	U. Katayama	Tyrrell	Lap 1 - Accident
25	(10)	R. Barrichello	Jordan	Lap 1 - Accident
26	(7)	E. Irvine	Jordan	Lap 1 - Accident

Non Qualifiers

27	B. Gachot		Pacific	1'24.908
28	P. Belmondo		Pacific	1'26.275

Fastest Laps
Qualifying: M. Schumacher - 1'18.258
Race: M. Schumacher - 1'20.881

FIA FORMULA 1 WORLD CHAMPIONSHIP - ROUND 11

Belgian Grand Prix
Spa Francorchamps - 28/08/94

Pos	Grid	Driver	Team	Race Time	Diff
1	(3)	D. Hill	Williams	1:28'47.170	
2	(8)	M. Hakkinen	McLaren	1:29'38.551	51.381
3	(6)	J. Verstappen	Benetton	1:29'57.623	1'10.453
4	(7)	D. Coulthard	Williams	1:30'32.957	1'45.787
5	(12)	M. Blundell	Tyrrell	1:28'59.728	1 Lap
6	(14)	G. Morbidelli	Arrows	1:29'09.393	1 Lap
7	(17)	O. Panis	Ligier	1:29'26.175	1 Lap
8	(10)	P. Martini	Minardi	1:29'49.362	1 Lap
9	(18)	M. Alboreto	Minardi	1:29'49.749	1 Lap
10	(16)	E. Bernard	Ligier	1:28'51.241	2 Laps
11	(25)	J. Gounon	Simtek	1:30'15.831	2 Laps
12	(20)	J. Herbert	Lotus	1:28'52.365	3 Laps
13	(4)	E. Irvine	Jordan	1:22'21.067	4 Laps

Retirements

Pos	Grid	Driver	Team	Lap-Retirement
14	(24)	C. Fittipaldi	Arrows	Lap 34 - Engine
15	(21)	D. Brabham	Simtek	Lap 30 - Wheel
16	(15)	A. de Cesaris	Sauber	Lap 28 - Throttle
17	(13)	M. Brundle	McLaren	Lap 25 - Accident
18	(1)	R. Barrichello	Jordan	Lap 20 - Accident
19	(23)	U. Katayama	Tyrrell	Lap 19 - Engine
20	(26)	P. Adams	Lotus	Lap 16 - Accident
21	(11)	G. Berger	Ferrari	Lap 12 - Engine
22	(19)	P. Alliot	Larrousse	Lap 12 - Engine
23	(9)	H.H. Frentzen	Sauber	Lap 11 - Gearbox
24	(22)	E. Comas	Larrousse	Lap 4 - Engine
25	(5)	J. Alesi	Ferrari	Lap 3 - Engine

Disqualified

26	(2)	M. Schumacher	Benetton	Undersized Skidblock

Non Qualifiers

27	B. Gachot	Pacific	2'34.582
28	P. Belmondo	Pacific	2'35.729

Fastest Laps
Qualifying: R. Barrichello - 2'21.163
Race: D. Hill - 1'57.117

FIA FORMULA 1 WORLD CHAMPIONSHIP - ROUND 12

Italian Grand Prix
Monza - 11/09/94

Pos	Grid	Driver	Team	Race Time	Diff
1	(3)	D. Hill	Williams	1:18'02.754	
2	(2)	G. Berger	Ferrari	1:18'07.684	4.930
3	(7)	M. Hakkinen	McLaren	1:18'28.394	25.640
4	(16)	R. Barrichello	Jordan	1:18'63.388	50.634
5	(15)	M. Brundle	McLaren	1:19'28.329	1'25.575
6	(5)	D. Coulthard	Williams	1:16'36.369	DNF
7	(12)	E. Bernard	Ligier	1:18'06.491	1 Lap
8	(24)	E. Comas	Larrousse	1:18'23.828	1 Lap
9	(20)	J.J. Lehto	Benetton	1:19'00.339	1 Lap
10	(6)	O. Panis	Ligier	1:18'33.332	2 Laps

Retirements

Pos	Grid	Driver	Team	Lap-Retirement
11	(26)	D. Brabham	Simtek	Lap 47 - Puncture
12	(14)	U. Katayama	Tyrrell	Lap 46 - Brakes
13	(19)	C. Fittipaldi	Arrows	Lap 44 - Engine
14	(9)	E. Irvine	Jordan	Lap 42 - Engine
15	(21)	M. Blundell	Tyrrell	Lap 40 - Brakes
16	(18)	P. Martini	Minardi	Lap 31 - Accident
17	(22)	M. Alboreto	Minardi	Lap 29 - Gearbox
18	(11)	H.H. Frentzen	Sauber	Lap 23 - Engine
19	(8)	A. de Cesaris	Sauber	Lap 21 - Engine
20	(25)	J. Gounon	Simtek	Lap 21 - Gearbox
21	(23)	Y. Dalmas	Larrousse	Lap 19 - Accident
22	(1)	J. Alesi	Ferrari	Lap 15 - Gearbox
23	(4)	J. Herbert	Lotus	Lap 14 - Engine
24	(10)	J. Verstappen	Benetton	Lap 1 - Accident
25	(17)	G. Morbidelli	Arrows	Lap 1 - Accident
26	(13)	A. Zanardi	Lotus	Lap 1 - Accident

Non Qualifiers

27	B. Gachot		Pacific	1'31.549
28	P. Belmondo		Pacific	1'32.035

Fastest Laps
Qualifying: J. Alesi - 1'23.844
Race: D. Hill - 1'25.930

FIA FORMULA 1 WORLD CHAMPIONSHIP - ROUND 13

Portuguese Grand Prix
Estoril - 25/09/94

Pos	Grid	Driver	Team	Race Time	Diff
1	(2)	D. Hill	Williams	1:41'10.165	
2	(3)	D. Coulthard	Williams	1:41'10.768	0.603
3	(4)	M. Hakkinen	McLaren	1:41'30.358	20.193
4	(8)	R. Barrichello	Jordan	1:41'38.168	28.003
5	(10)	J. Verstappen	Benetton	1:41'39.550	29.385
6	(7)	M. Brundle	McLaren	1:42'02.867	52.702
7	(13)	E. Irvine	Jordan	1:41'16.394	1 Lap
8	(11)	C. Fittipaldi	Arrows	1:41'20.632	1 Lap
9	(16)	G. Morbidelli	Arrows	1:41'26.415	1 Lap
10	(21)	E. Bernard	Ligier	1:42'10.305	1 Lap
11	(20)	J. Herbert	Lotus	1:42'21.674	1 Lap
12	(18)	P. Martini	Minardi	1:42'02.548	2 Laps
13	(19)	M. Alboreto	Minardi	1:42'03.256	2 Laps
14	(23)	Y. Dalmas	Larrousse	1:42'04.177	2 Laps
15	(26)	J. Gounon	Simtek	1:41'36.488	4 Laps
16	(25)	P. Adams	Lotus	1:41'59.533	4 Laps

Retirements

Pos	Grid	Driver	Team	Lap-Retirement
17	(12)	M. Blundell	Tyrrell	Lap 62 - Engine
18	(14)	J.J. Lehto	Benetton	Lap 61 - Accident
19	(17)	A. de Cesaris	Sauber	Lap 55 - Gearbox
20	(5)	J. Alesi	Ferrari	Lap 39 - Accident
21	(24)	D. Brabham	Simtek	Lap 37 - Accident
22	(9)	H.H. Frentzen	Sauber	Lap 32 - Transmission
23	(22)	E. Comas	Larrousse	Lap 28 - Accident
24	(6)	U. Katayama	Tyrrell	Lap 27 - Gearbox
25	(1)	G. Berger	Ferrari	Lap 8 - Transmission

Disqualified

26	(15)	O. Panis	Ligier	Undersized Skidblock

Non Qualifiers

27	B. Gachot	Pacific	1'27.385
28	P. Belmondo	Pacific	1'29.000

Fastest Laps
Qualifying: G. Berger - 1'20.608
Race: D. Coulthard - 1'22.446

FIA FORMULA 1 WORLD CHAMPIONSHIP - ROUND 14

European Grand Prix
Jerez - 16/10/94

Pos	Grid	Driver	Team	Race Time	Diff
1	(1)	M. Schumacher	Benetton	1:40'26.689	
2	(2)	D. Hill	Williams	1:40'51.378	24.689
3	(9)	M. Hakkinen	McLaren	1:41'36.337	1'09.648
4	(10)	E. Irvine	Jordan	1:41'45.135	1'18.446
5	(6)	G. Berger	Ferrari	1:40'31.515	1 Lap
6	(4)	H.H. Frentzen	Sauber	1:40'38.757	1 Lap
7	(13)	U. Katayama	Tyrrell	1:40'38.910	1 Lap
8	(7)	J. Herbert	Ligier	1:40'51.752	1 Lap
9	(11)	O. Panis	Ligier	1:40'52.310	1 Lap
10	(16)	J. Alesi	Ferrari	1:40'52.887	1 Lap
11	(8)	G. Morbidelli	Arrows	1:41'11.272	1 Lap
12	(5)	R. Barrichello	Jordan	1:41'20.659	1 Lap
13	(14)	M. Blundell	Tyrrell	1:41'24.708	1 Lap
14	(20)	M. Alboreto	Minardi	1:41'05.095	2 Laps
15	(17)	P. Martini	Minardi	1:41'18.363	2 Laps
16	(21)	A. Zanardi	Lotus	1:41'20.538	2 Laps
17	(19)	C. Fittipaldi	Arrows	1:40'48.342	3 Laps
18	(22)	E. Bernard	Lotus	1:40'56.166	3 Laps
19	(26)	D. Schiattarella	Simtek	1:40'39.708	5 Laps

Retirements

Pos	Grid	Driver	Team	Lap-Retirement
20	(3)	N. Mansell	Williams	Lap 48 - Gearbox
21	(25)	D. Brabham	Simtek	Lap 43 - Engine
22	(18)	A. de Cesaris	Sauber	Lap 38 - Accelerator
23	(23)	E. Comas	Larrousse	Lap 38 - Electrics
24	(12)	J. Verstappen	Benetton	Lap 16 - Accident
25	(24)	H. Noda	Larrousse	Lap 11 - Gearbox
26	(15)	M. Brundle	McLaren	Lap 9 - Engine

Non Qualifiers

27	B. Gachot	Pacific	1'29.488
28	P. Belmondo	Pacific	1'30.234

Fastest Laps
Qualifying: M. Schumacher - 1'22.762
Race: M. Schumacher - 1'25.040

FIA FORMULA 1 WORLD CHAMPIONSHIP - ROUND 15

Japanese Grand Prix
Suzuka - 06/11/94

Pos	Grid	Driver	Team	Race Time	Diff
1	(2)	D. Hill	Williams	1:55'53.632	
2	(1)	M. Schumacher	Benetton	1:55'56.897	3.365
3	(7)	J. Alesi	Ferrari	1:56'46.877	52.045
4	(4)	N. Mansell	Williams	1:56'49.606	56.074
5	(6)	E. Irvine	Jordan	1:57'35.639	1'42.107
6	(3)	H.H. Frentzen	Sauber	1:57'53.395	1'59.863
7	(8)	M. Hakkinen	McLaren	1:57'56.517	2'02.985
8	(18)	C. Fittipaldi	Arrows	1:55'51.227	1 Lap
9	(22)	E. Comas	Larrousse	1:57'07.255	1 Lap
10	(25)	M. Salo	Lotus	1:57'38.177	1 Lap
11	(19)	O. Panis	Ligier	1:57'41.269	1 Lap
12	(24)	D. Brabham	Simtex	1:57'10.846	2 Laps
13	(17)	A. Zanardi	Lotus	1:57'17.049	2 Laps

Retirements

Pos	Grid	Driver	Team	Lap-Retirement
14	(13)	M. Blundell	Tyrrell	Lap 27 - Engine
15	(10)	R. Barrichello	Jordan	Lap 17 - Gearbox
16	(9)	M. Brundle	McLaren	Lap 14 - Accident
17	(12)	G. Morbidelli	Arrows	Lap 14 - Accident
18	(11)	G. Berger	Ferrari	Lap 11 - Electrics
19	(20)	F. Lagorce	Ligier	Lap 11 - Accident
20	(16)	P. Martini	Minardi	Lap 11 - Accident
21	(21)	M. Alboreto	Minardi	Lap 11 - Accident
22	(5)	J. Herbert	Benetton	Lap 4 - Accident
23	(14)	U. Katayama	Tyrrell	Lap 4 - Accident
24	(26)	T. Inoue	Simtek	Lap 4 - Accident
25	(23)	H. Noda	Larrousse	Lap 1 - Electrics
26	(15)	J. Lehto	Sauber	Lap 1 - Engine

Non Qualifiers

27	B. Gachot	Pacific	1'46.374
28	P. Belmondo	Pacific	1'46.629

Fastest Laps
Qualifying lap: M. Schumacher - 1'37.209
Race lap: D. Hill - 1'56.597

FIA FORMULA 1 WORLD CHAMPIONSHIP - ROUND 16

Australian Grand Prix
Adelaide - 13/11/94

Pos	Grid	Driver	Team	Race Time	Diff
1	(1)	N. Mansell	Williams	1:47'51.480	
2	(11)	G. Berger	Ferrari	1:47'53.991	2.511
3	(9)	M. Brundle	McLaren	1:48'43.953	52.487
4	(5)	R. Barrichello	Jordan	1:49'02.010	1'10.530
5	(12)	O. Panis	Ligier	1:47'52.837	1 Lap
6	(8)	J Alesi	Ferrari	1:47'54.719	1 Lap
7	(10)	H.H. Frentzen	Sauber	1:48'14.255	1 Lap
8	(19)	C. Fittipaldi	Arrows	1:49'11.528	1 Lap
9	(18)	P. Martini	Minardi	1:48'30.092	2 Laps
10	(17)	J.J. Lehto	Sauber	1:48'54.886	2 Laps
11	(20)	F. Lagorce	Ligier	1:49'02.814	2 Laps
12	(4)	M. Hakkinen	McLaren	1:42'04.160	5 Laps

Retirements

Pos	Grid	Driver	Team	Lap-Retirement
13	(16)	M. Alboreto	Minardi	Lap 70 - Suspension
14	(13)	M. Blundell	Tyrrell	Lap 67 - Accident
15	(25)	J.D. Deletraz	Larrousse	Lap 57 - Gearbox
16	(22)	M. Salo	Lotus	Lap 50 - Electrics
17	(24)	D. Brabham	Simtek	Lap 50 - Engine
18	(14)	A. Zanardi	Lotus	Lap 41 - Throttle
19	(2)	M. Schumacher	Benetton	Lap 36 - Accident
20	(3)	D. Hill	Williams	Lap 36 - Accident
21	(26)	M. Schiattarella	Simtek	Lap 22 - Gearbox
22	(15)	U. Katayama	Tyrrell	Lap 20 - Accident
23	(23)	H. Noda	Larrousse	Lap 19 - Oil Leak
24	(21)	G. Morbidelli	Arrows	Lap 18 - Oil Pump
25	(6)	E. Irvine	Jordan	Lap 16 - Accident
26	(7)	J. Herbert	Benetton	Lap 14 - Gearbox

Non Qualifiers

27	P. Belmondo	Pacific	1'24.087
28	B. Gachot	Pacific	7'40.317

Fastest Laps
Qualifying: N. Mansell - 1'16.179
Race: M. Schumacher - 1'17.140

1994 Drivers' World Championship

1	Michael Schumacher	Germany	92
2	Damon Hill	Great Britain	91
3	Gerhard Berger	Austria	41
4	Mika Hakkinen	Finland	26
5	Jean Alesi	France	24
6	Rubens Barrichello	Brazil	19
7	Martin Brundle	Great Britain	16
8	David Coulthard	Great Britain	14
9	Nigel Mansell	Great Britain	13
10	Jos Verstappen	Holland	10
11	Olivier Panis	France	9
12	Mark Blundell	Great Britain	8
13	Heinz-Harald Frentzen	Germany	7
14=	Christian Fittipaldi	Brazil	6
14=	Eddie Irvine	Great Britain	6
14=	Nicola Larini	Italy	6
17	Ukyo Katayama	Japan	5
18=	Eric Bernard	France	4
18=	Andrea de Cesaris	Italy	4
18=	Pierluigi Martini	Italy	4
18=	Karl Wendlinger	Austria	4
22	Gianni Morbidelli	Italy	3
23	Erik Comas	France	2
24=	Michele Alboreto	Brazil	1
24=	J.J. Lehto	Finland	1

1994 Constructors' World Championship

1	Williams-Renault	118
2	Benetton-Ford	103
3	Ferrari	71
4	McLaren-Peugeot	42
5	Jordan-Hart	28
6=	Ligier-Renault	13
6=	Tyrrell-Yamaha	13
8	Sauber-Mercedes	12
9	Arrows-Footwork Ford	9
10	Minardi-Ford	5
11	Larrousse-Ford	2

1994 Teams

*Rubens Barrichello leads the field away on the pace lap,
Belgian Grand Prix 1994*

ARROWS

Full name: Footwork Arrows Ford
Address: Arrows Grand Prix International
39 Barton Road, Water Eaton Industrial Estate, Bletchley,
Milton Keynes, Bucks, MK2 3HW

Tele: +44 (0)908 270047
Fax: +44 (0)908 274123

Managing Director & Team Principal: Jackie Oliver
Financial Director: Alan Rees
Technical Director: Alan Jenkins
Team Manager: John Wickham
Chief Mechanic: Ken Sibley

Engine: Ford HB V8
Chassis: Footwork FA15

1994 GRAND PRIX RECORD

	Grand Prix	Driver	Pos	Driver	Pos	Pts
1	Brazilian	Fittipaldi	Ret	Morbidelli	Ret	0
2	Pacific	Fittipaldi	4th	Morbidelli	Ret	3
3	San Marino	Fittipaldi	Ret	Morbidelli	Ret	0
4	Monaco	Fittipaldi	Ret	Morbidelli	Ret	0
5	Spanish	Fittipaldi	Ret	Morbidelli	Ret	0
6	Canadian	Fittipaldi	Dis	Morbidelli	Ret	0
7	French	Fittipaldi	8th	Morbidelli	Ret	0
8	British	Fittipaldi	9th	Morbidelli	Ret	0
9	German	Fittipaldi	4th	Morbidelli	5th	5
10	Hungarian	Fittipaldi	14th	Morbidelli	Ret	0
11	Belgian	Fittipaldi	Ret	Morbidelli	6th	1
12	Italian	Fittipaldi	Ret	Morbidelli	Ret	0
13	Portuguese	Fittipaldi	8th	Morbidelli	9th	0
14	European	Fittipaldi	17th	Morbidelli	11th	0
15	Japanese	Fittipaldi	8th	Morbidelli	Ret	0
16	Australian	Fittipaldi	8th	Morbidelli	Ret	0

Races: 16
Wins: 0
Pole positions: 0
Points: 9
Constructors Championship: 9th

Drivers Championship
Christian Fittipaldi: =14th (6)
Gianni Morbidelli: 22nd (3)

COMPLETE GRAND PRIX RECORD
First race: Brazilian - Rio de Janeiro - 29/01/78
Total races: 255
Pole positions: 1
Wins: 0
Highest finish: 2nd
Top six finishes: 66
Points: 135
Most points in a season: 23 - 1988
Highest Constructors World Championship position:
=4th 1988
Highest Drivers World Championship position: =7th 1988
(Derek Warwick)

Top six finishes: 1978: US (West) (6), Mon (6), Swe (2),
Can (4) 1979: Bel (5), Mon (6), Ger (6), Dut (6) 1980: Bra
(6), SA (6), US (West) (2), Mon (4) 1981: Bra (3), SM (2)
1982: Can (5), Dut (6), Ger (6), Aus (6) 1983: Bra (6), US
(West) (5), SM (6) 1984: Bra (6), SM (5), Aus (5/6) 1985:
SM (2), Ger (4), Eur (6), SA (5/6), Aust (6) 1986: Aus (6)
1987: Bel (4), US (6), GB (5), Hun (6), Por (6), Mex (4)
1988: Bra (4), Mon (4), Mex (5/6), GB (6), Bel (5/6), It (3/4),
Por (4) 1989: Bra (5), SM (5), US (3), Ger (6), Hun (5), Bel
(6), Jap (6) 1990: Mon (5) 1992: Bra (6), Sp (5), SM (5), Por
(6) 1993: GB (6), Hun (4) 1994: Pac (4), Ger (4/5), Bel (6)

Constructors Championship 1978-1994: 1978: =9th (11)
1979: 9th (5) 1980: =7th (11) 1981: =8th (10) 1982: 11th (5)
1983: 10th (4) 1984: 9th (6) 1985: 8th (14) 1986: 10th (1)
1987: =6th (11) 1988: =4th (23) 1989: 7th (13) 1990: =9th
(2) 1991: - (0) 1992: =7th (6) 1993: 9th (4) 1994: 9th (9)

BENETTON

Full name: Mild Seven Benetton Ford
Address: Benetton Formula Limited
Whiteways Technical Centre, Enstone, Chipping Norton,
Oxon, OX7 4EE

Tele: +44 (0)608 678000
Fax: +44 (0)608 678609

Managing Director: Flavio Briatore
Engineering Director: Tom Walkinshaw
Technical Director: Ross Brawn
Team Manager: Joan Villadelprat
Chief Mechanic: Mick Ainsley Cowlishaw

Engine: Ford Zetec-R V8
Chassis: Benetton B194

1994 Test driver: Jos Verstappen

1994 GRAND PRIX RECORD

Grand Prix	Driver	Pos	Driver	Pos	Pts
1 Brazilian	Schumacher	1st	Verstappen	Ret	10
2 Pacific	Schumacher	1st	Verstappen	Ret	10
3 San Marino	Schumacher	1st	Lehto	Ret	10
4 Monaco	Schumacher	1st	Lehto	7th	10
5 Spanish	Schumacher	2nd	Lehto	Ret	6
6 Canadian	Schumacher	1st	Lehto	6th	11
7 French	Schumacher	1st	Verstappen	Ret	10
8 British	Schumacher	Dis	Verstappen	8th	0*
9 German	Schumacher	Ret	Verstappen	Ret	0
10 Hungarian	Schumacher	1st	Verstappen	3rd	14
11 Belgian	Schumacher	Dis	Verstappen	3rd	4
12 Italian	Lehto	9th	Verstappen	Ret	0
13 Portuguese	Lehto	Ret	Verstappen	5th	2
14 European	Schumacher	1st	Verstappen	Ret	10
15 Japanese	Schumacher	2nd	Herbert	Ret	6
16 Australian	Schumacher	Ret	Herbert	Ret	0

Races: 16
Wins: 8
Pole positions: 6
Points: 103
1994 Constructors Championship: 2nd

1994 Drivers Championship
Michael Schumacher: 1st (92)
Jos Verstappen: 10th (10)
J.J. Lehto: =24th (1)

COMPLETE GRAND PRIX RECORD
As Toleman - 1981-85
First race: Italian - Monza - 13/09/81
Total races: 57
Pole positions: 0
Wins: 0
Highest finish: 2nd
Points: 26

As Benetton - 1986-94
First race: Brazilian - Rio de Janeiro - 23/03/86
Total races: 144
Pole positions: 9
Wins: 15
First win: Mexican - Mexico City - 12/10/86
Points: 500.5
Most wins in a season: 8 - 1994
Most points in a season: 103 - 1994
Highest Constructors World Championship position: 2nd - 1994
Highest Drivers World Championship position: Winners 1994 (Michael Schumacher)

Grand Prix victories: 1986: Mex (1) 1989: Jap (1) 1990: Jap, Aust (2) 1991: Can (1) 1992: Bel (1) 1993: Por (1) 1994: Bra, Pac, SM, Mon, Can, Fra, Hun, Eur (8)

Constructors Championship 1981-1994: (As Toleman) 1981: - (0) 1982: - (0) 1983: 9th (10) 1984: 7th (16) 1985: - (0) (As Benetton) 1986: 6th (19) 1987: 5th (28) 1988: 3rd (39) 1989: 4th (39) 1990: 3rd (71) 1991: 4th (38.5) 1992: 3rd (91) 1993: 3rd (72) 1994: 2nd (103)

FERRARI

Full name: Scuderia Ferrari
Address: Scuderia Ferrari
Via Alberto Ascari 55/57, 41053 Maranello (MO), Italy

Tele: +39 536 949111
Fax: +39 536 946488

President: Luca di Montezemolo
Chief Designer: John Barnard
Sporting Director: Jean Todt

Engine: Ferrari V12
Chassis: Ferrari 412 T1 - 412 T1/B

1994 Test Driver: Nicola Larini

1994 GRAND PRIX RECORD

Grand Prix	Driver	Pos	Driver	Pos	Pts
1 Brazilian	Alesi	3rd	Berger	Ret	4
2 Pacific	Larini	Ret	Berger	2nd	6
3 San Marino	Larini	2nd	Berger	Ret	6
4 Monaco	Alesi	5th	Berger	3rd	6
5 Spanish	Alesi	4th	Berger	Ret	3
6 Canadian	Alesi	3rd	Berger	4th	7
7 French	Alesi	Ret	Berger	3rd	4
8 British	Alesi	2nd	Berger	Ret	6
9 German	Alesi	Ret	Berger	1st	10
10 Hungarian	Alesi	Ret	Berger	12th	0
11 Belgian	Alesi	Ret	Berger	Ret	0
12 Italian	Alesi	Ret	Berger	2nd	6
13 Portuguese	Alesi	Ret	Berger	Ret	0
14 European	Alesi	10th	Berger	5th	2
15 Japanese	Alesi	3rd	Berger	Ret	4
16 Australian	Alesi	6th	Berger	2nd	7

Races: 16
Wins: 1
Pole positions: 3
Points: 71
1994 Constructors Championship: 3rd

1994 Drivers Championship
Gerhard Berger: 3rd (41)
Jean Alesi: 5th (24)
Nicola Larini: =14th (6)

COMPLETE GRAND PRIX RECORD
First race: Monaco - Monte Carlo - 21/05/50
Races: 537*
Pole positions: 113
Wins: 104
First win: British - Silverstone - 14/07/51
Points: 1850.5
Most wins in a season: 7 - 1952, 1953
Most points in a season: 113 - 1979
Highest Constructors World Championship position:
Winners: 1961, 1964, 1975, 1976, 1977, 1979, 1982, 1983
Highest Drivers World Championship position: Winners:
1952 (Alberto Ascari), 1953 (Alberto Ascari), 1956 (Juan
Manuel Fangio), 1958 (Mike Hawthorn), 1961 (Phil Hill),
1964 (John Surtees), 1975 (Niki Lauda), 1977 (Niki Lauda),
1979 (Jody Scheckter)

Grand Prix victories: 1951: GB, Ger, It (3) 1952: Swi, Bel,
Fr, GB, Ger, Dut, It (7) 1953: Arg, Dut, Bel, Fr, GB, Ger,
Swi (7) 1954: GB, Sp (2) 1955: Mon (1) 1956: Arg, Bel, Fr,
GB, Ger (5) 1958: Fr, GB (2) 1959: Fr, Ger (2) 1960: It (1)
1961: Dut, Bel, Fr, GB, It (5) 1963: Ger (1) 1964: Ger, Aus,

It (3) 1966: Bel, It (2) 1968: Fr (1) 1970: Aus, It, Can, Mex (4) 1971: SA, Dut (2) 1972: Ger (1) 1974: Sp, Dut, Ger (3) 1975: Mon, Bel, Swe, Fr, It, US (6) 1976: Bra, SA, US (West), Bel, Mon, GB (6) 1977: Bra, SA, Ger, Dut (4) 1978: Bra, US (West), GB, US (East), Can (5) 1979: SA, US (West), Bel, Mon, It, US (East) (6) 1981: Mon, Sp (2) 1982: SM, Dut, Ger (3) 1983: SM, Can, Ger, Dut (4) 1984: Bel (1) 1985: Can, Ger (2) 1987: Jap, Aust (2) 1988: It (1) 1989 Bra, Hun, Por (3) 1990: Bra, Mex, Fr, GB, Por, Sp (6) 1994: Ger (1)

Constructors Championship 1958-1994: 1958: 2nd (40/57) 1959: 2nd (32/38) 1960: 3rd (26/27) 1961: 1st (40/52) 1962: =5th (18) 1963: 4th (26) 1964: 1st (45/49) 1965: 4th (26/27) 1966: 2nd (31/32) 1967: =4th (20) 1968: 4th (32) 1969: =5th (7) 1970: 2nd (52/55) 1971: =3rd (33) 1972: 4th (33) 1973: =6th (12) 1974: 2nd (65) 1975: 1st (72.5) 1976: 1st (83) 1977: 1st (95/97) 1978: 2nd (58) 1979: 1st (113) 1980: 10th (8) 1981: 5th (34) 1982: 1st (74) 1983: 1st (89) 1984: 2nd (57.5) 1985: 2nd (82) 1986: 4th (37) 1987: 4th (53) 1988: 2nd (65) 1989: 3rd (59) 1990: 2nd (110) 1991: 3rd (55.5) 1992: 4th (21) 1993: 4th (28) 1994: 3rd (71)

* Including the 1952 Indianapolis 500

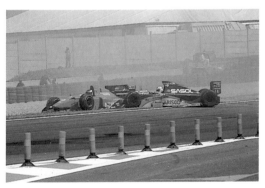

Jean Alesi hits Rubens Barrichello,
French Grand Prix 1994

JORDAN

Full name: Sasol Jordan Hart
Address: Jordan Grand Prix Limited
Buckingham Road, Silverstone, Northamptonshire, NN12
8TJ

Tele: +44 (0)327 857153
Fax: +44 (0)327 858120

Managing Director: Eddie Jordan
Chief Designer: Steve Nichols
Chief Engineer: Gary Anderson
Team Manager: John "Johnboy" Walton

Engine: Hart V10, 1035
Chassis: Jordan 194

1994 Test Drivers: Vitorio Zoboli, Kelvin Burt

1994 GRAND PRIX RECORD

Grand Prix	Driver	Pos	Driver	Pos	Pts
1 Brazilian	Barrichello	4th	Irvine	Ret	3
2 Pacific	Barrichello	3rd	Suzuki	Ret	4
3 San Marino	Barrichello	DNQ	de Cesaris	Ret	0
4 Monaco	Barrichello	Ret	de Cesaris	4th	3
5 Spanish	Barrichello	Ret	Irvine	6th	1
6 Canadian	Barrichello	7th	Irvine	Ret	0
7 French	Barrichello	Ret	Irvine	Ret	0
8 British	Barrichello	4th	Irvine	Ret	3
9 German	Barrichello	Ret	Irvine	Ret	0
10 Hungarian	Barrichello	Ret	Irvine	Ret	0
11 Belgian	Barrichello	Ret	Irvine	13th	0
12 Italian	Barrichello	4th	Irvine	Ret	3
13 Portuguese	Barrichello	4th	Irvine	7th	3
14 European	Barrichello	12th	Irvine	4th	3
15 Japanese	Barrichello	Ret	Irvine	5th	2
16 Australian	Barrichello	4th	Irvine	Ret	3

Races: 16
Wins: 0
Pole positions: 1
Points: 28
1994 Constructors Championship: 5th

1994 Drivers Championship
Rubens Barrichello: 6th (19)
Eddie Irvine: =14th (6)
Andrea de Cesaris: =18th* (4)

* Includes 1 point scored in 11 races with Sauber

COMPLETE GRAND PRIX RECORD
First race: United States - Phoenix - 10/03/91
Total races: 64
Pole positions: 1
Wins: 0
Highest finish: 3rd
Top six finishes: 20
Points: 45
Most points in a season: 28 - 1994
Highest Constructors World Championship position: 5th
- 1991, 1994
Highest Drivers World Championship position: 6th 1994
(Rubens Barrichello)

Top six finishes: 1991: Can (4/5), Mex (4), Fr (6), GB (6),
Ger (5/6) 1992: Aust (6) 1993: Jap (5/6) 1994: Bra (4), Pac
(3), Mon (4), Sp (6), GB (4), It (4), Por (4), Eur (4), Jap (5),
Aust (4)

Constructors Championship 1991-1994: 1991: 5th (13)
1992: =11th (1) 1993: =10th (3) 1994: 5th (28)

LARROUSSE

Full name: Tourtel Larrousse F1
Address: Larrousse F1
Signes ZE, BP 702, 83030 Toulon, CDX 9, France

Tele: +33 943 28888
Fax: +33 943 28141

Team Principal: Gerard Larrousse
Designers: Tino Belli, Tim Holloway, Robin Herd
Crew Chief: Alain Marguet

Engine: Ford HB V8
Chassis: Larrousse LH 94

1994 GRAND PRIX RECORD

Grand Prix	Driver	Pos	Driver	Pos	Pts
1 Brazilian	Beretta	Ret	Comas	9th	0
2 Pacific	Beretta	Ret	Comas	6th	1
3 San Marino	Beretta	Ret	Comas	Ret	0
4 Monaco	Beretta	8th	Comas	10th	0
5 Spanish	Beretta	Ret	Comas	Ret	0
6 Canadian	Beretta	Ret	Comas	Ret	0
7 French	Beretta	Ret	Comas	Ret	0
8 British	Beretta	14th	Comas	Ret	0
9 German	Beretta	7th	Comas	6th	1
10 Hungarian	Beretta	9th	Comas	8th	0
11 Belgian	Alliot	Ret	Comas	Ret	0
12 Italian	Dalmas	Ret	Comas	8th	0
13 Portuguese	Dalmas	14th	Comas	Ret	0
14 European	Noda	Ret	Comas	Ret	0
15 Japanese	Noda	Ret	Comas	9th	0
16 Australian	Noda	Ret	Deletraz	Ret	0

Races: 16
Wins: 0
Pole positions: 0
Points: 2
1994 Constructors Championship: 11th

1994 Drivers Championship
Erik Comas: 23rd (2)

COMPLETE GRAND PRIX RECORD
First race: San Marino - Imola - 03/05/87
Total races: 126
Pole positions: 0
Wins: 0
Highest finish: 3rd
Top six finishes: 18
Points: 23
Most points in a season: 11 - 1990
Highest Constructors World Championship position: 6th
- 1990
Highest Drivers World Championship position: =10th -
1990 (Aguri Suzuki)

Top six finishes: 1987: Ger (6), Sp (6), Mex (6), Aust (5)*
1989: Sp (6) 1990: Mon (6), GB (4/6), Hun (6), Sp (6), Jap
(3) 1991: US (6), Mex (6) 1992: Mon (6) 1993: SM (5), It (6)
1994: Pac (6), Ger (6)

Constructors Championship: 1987: 9th (3) 1988: - (0)
1989: =15th (1) 1990: 6th (11) 1991: 11th (2) 1992: =11th
(1) 1993: =10th (3) 1994: 11th (2)

* Driver (Yannick Dalmas) not entered in Championship,
ineligible for points

LIGIER

Full name: Ligier Gitanes Blondes
Address: Ligier F1
Technopole du Circuit, 58470 Magny-Cours, France

Tele: + 33 866 06200
Fax: + 33 862 12296

Sporting Director: Cesare Fiorio
Technical Director: Frank Dernie
Operations & Financial Director: Bruno Michel
Race Engineers: Gilles, Alegoet & Steve Clark

Engine: Renault V10
Chassis: Ligier JS39

1994 GRAND PRIX RECORD

	Grand Prix	Driver	Pos	Driver	Pos	Pts
1	Brazilian	Bernard	Ret	Panis	11th	0
2	Pacific	Bernard	10th	Panis	9th	0
3	San Marino	Bernard	12th	Panis	11th	0
4	Monaco	Bernard	Ret	Panis	9th	0
5	Spanish	Bernard	8th	Panis	7th	0
6	Canadian	Bernard	13th	Panis	12th	0
7	French	Bernard	Ret	Panis	Ret	0
8	British	Bernard	13th	Panis	12th	0
9	German	Bernard	3rd	Panis	2nd	10
10	Hungarian	Bernard	10th	Panis	6th	1
11	Belgian	Bernard	10th	Panis	7th	0
12	Italian	Bernard	7th	Panis	10th	0
13	Portuguese	Bernard	10th	Panis	Ret	0
14	European	Herbert	8th	Panis	9th	0
15	Japanese	Lagorce	Ret	Panis	11th	0
16	Australian	Lagorce	11th	Panis	5th	2

Races: 16
Wins: 0
Pole positions: 0
Points: 13
1994 Constructors Championship: =6th

1994 Drivers Championship
Olivier Panis: 11th (9)
Eric Bernard: =18th (4)

COMPLETE GRAND PRIX RECORD
First race: Brazilian - Interlagos - 25/01/76
Total races: 293
Wins: 8
Pole positions: 9
First win: Swedish - Anderstorp - 19/06/77
Most wins in a season: 3 - 1979
Points: 349
Most points in a season: 66 - 1980

Highest Constructors World Championship position: 2nd - 1980
Highest Drivers World Championship position: 4th 1979 (Jacques Laffite), 4th 1980 (Jacques Laffite), 1981 (Jacques Laffite)

Grand Prix victories: 1977: Swe (1) 1979: Arg, Bra, Sp (3) 1980: Bel, Ger (2) 1981: Aus, Can (2)

Constructors Championship 1976-1994: 1976 =5th (20) 1977: 8th (18) 1978: 6th (19) 1979: 3rd (61) 1980: 2nd (66) 1981: 4th (44) 1982: 8th (20) 1983: - (0) 1984: 10th (3) 1985: 6th (23) 1986: 5th (29) 1987: =11th (1) 1988: - (0) 1989: =13th (3) 1990: - (0), 1991: - (0) 1992: =7th (6) 1993: 5th (23) 1994: =6th (13)

LOTUS

Full name: Team Lotus
Address: Team Lotus International
Ketteringham Hall, Wymondham, Norfolk, NR18 9RS

Tele: +44 (0)603 811190
Fax: +44 (0)603 810467

Managing director: Peter Collins
Team manager: Trevor Foster
Technical Director: Peter Wright
Chief Designer: Chris Murphy
Chief Mechanic: Paul Diggins

Engine: Mugen Honda ZA5C V10
Chassis: Lotus 107C

1994 GRAND PRIX RECORD

	Grand Prix	Driver	Pos	Driver	Pos	Pts
1	Brazilian	Lamy	10th	Herbert	7th	0
2	Pacific	Lamy	8th	Herbert	7th	0
3	San Marino	Lamy	Ret	Herbert	10th	0
4	Monaco	Lamy	11th	Herbert	Ret	0
5	Spanish	Zanardi	9th	Herbert	Ret	0
6	Canadian	Zanardi	Ret	Herbert	8th	0
7	French	Zanardi	Ret	Herbert	7th	0
8	British	Zanardi	Ret	Herbert	11th	0
9	German	Zanardi	Ret	Herbert	Ret	0
10	Hungarian	Zanardi	13th	Herbert	Ret	0
11	Belgian	Adams	Ret	Herbert	12th	0
12	Italian	Zanardi	Ret	Herbert	Ret	0
13	Portuguese	Adams	16th	Herbert	11th	0
14	European	Zanardi	16th	Bernard	18th	0
15	Japanese	Zanardi	13th	Salo	10th	0
16	Australian	Zanardi	Ret	Salo	Ret	0

Races: 16
Wins: 0
Pole positions: 0
Points: 0
1994 Constructors Championship: No position

COMPLETE GRAND PRIX RECORD
GP Debut: Monaco - Monte Carlo - 18/05/58
Races: 491
Pole positions: 107
Wins: 79
First win: Monaco - Monte Carlo - 29/05/60

Points: 1368
Most wins in a season: 8 - 1978
Most points in a season: 96 - 1973

Highest Constructors World Championship position:
Winners: 1963, 1965, 1968, 1970, 1972, 1973, 1978
Highest driver World Championship position: Winners:
1963 (Jim Clark), 1965 (Jim Clark), 1968 (Graham Hill),
1970 (Jochen Rindt), 1972 (Emerson Fittipaldi), 1978 (Mario
Andretti)

Grand Prix victories: 1960: Mon, US (2) 1961: Mon, Ger,
US (3) 1962: Bel, GB, US (3) 1963: Bel, Dut, Fr, GB, It,
Mex, SA (7) 1964: Dut, Bel, GB (3) 1965: SA, Bel, Fr, GB,
Dut, Ger (6) 1966: US (1) 1967: Dut, GB, US, Mex (4) 1968:
SA, Sp, Mon, GB, Mex (5) 1969: Mon, US (2) 1970: Mon,
Dut, Fr, GB, Ger, US (6) 1972: Sp, Bel, GB, Aus, It (5) 1973:
Arg, Bra, Sp, Fr, Aus, It, US (7) 1974: Mon, Fr, It (3) 1976:
Jap (1) 1977: US (West), Sp, Bel, Fr, It (5) 1978: Arg, SA,
Bel, Sp, Fr, Ger, Aus, Dut (8) 1982: Aus (1) 1985: Por, SM,
Bel (3) 1986: Sp, Det (2) 1987: Mon, US (2)

Constructors Championship 1958-1994: 1958: 6th (3)
1959: 4th (5) 1960: 2nd (34/37) 1961: 2nd (32) 1962: 2nd
(36/38) 1963: 1st (54/74) 1964: 3rd (37/40) 1965: 1st (54/58)
1966: 6th (8) 1967: 2nd (44) 1968: 1st (62) 1969: 3rd (47)
1970: 1st (59) 1971: 5th (21) 1972: 1st (61) 1973: 1st (92/
96) 1974: 4th (42) 1975: 7th (9) 1976: 4th (29) 1977: 2nd
(62) 1978: 1st (86) 1979: 4th (39) 1980: 5th (14) 1981: 7th
(22) 1982: 5th (30) 1983: 8th (11) 1984: 3rd (47) 1985: =3rd
(71) 1986: 3rd (58) 1987: 3rd (64) 1988: 4th (23) 1989: 6th
(15) 1990: 8th (3) 1991: (3) 1992: 5th (13) 1993: =6th (12)
1994: - (0)

Constructors Championship second team: 1962: 8th (1)
1963: 8th (4) 1964: 8th (3) 1965: 8th (2) 1966: 5th (13)
1967: =8th (6) 1983: =12th (1)

MCLAREN

Full name: Marlboro McLaren Peugeot
Address: McLaren International Ltd
Woking Business Park, Albert Drive, Woking, Surrey, GU21
5JY

Tele: +44 (0)483 728211
Fax: +44 (0)483 720157

Managing Director: Ron Dennis
Technical Director: Neil Oatley
Team Co-ordinator: Jo Ramirez
Team Manager: Dave Ryan
Chief Mechanic: Paul Simpson

Engine: Peugeot A4/A6 V10
Chassis: McLaren MP4/9

1994 Test driver: Philippe Alliot

1994 GRAND PRIX RECORD

	Grand Prix	Driver	Pos	Driver	Pos	Pts
1	Brazilian	Hakkinen	Ret	Brundle	Ret	0
2	Pacific	Hakkinen	Ret	Brundle	Ret	0
3	San Marino	Hakkinen	3rd	Brundle	8th	4
4	Monaco	Hakkinen	Ret	Brundle	2nd	6
5	Spanish	Hakkinen	Ret	Brundle	Ret	0
6	Canadian	Hakkinen	Ret	Brundle	Ret	0
7	French	Hakkinen	Ret	Brundle	Ret	0
8	British	Hakkinen	3rd	Brundle	Ret	4
9	German	Hakkinen	Ret	Brundle	Ret	0
10	Hungarian	Alliot	Ret	Brundle	4th	3
11	Belgian	Hakkinen	2nd	Brundle	Ret	6
12	Italian	Hakkinen	3rd	Brundle	5th	6
13	Portuguese	Hakkinen	3rd	Brundle	6th	5
14	European	Hakkinen	3rd	Brundle	Ret	4
15	Japanese	Hakkinen	7th	Brundle	Ret	0
16	Australian	Hakkinen	12th	Brundle	3rd	4

Races: 16
Wins: 0
Pole positions: 0
Points: 42
1994 Constructors Championship: 4th

1994 Drivers Championship
Mika Hakkinen: 4th (26)
Martin Brundle: 7th (16)

COMPLETE GRAND PRIX RECORD:
First race: Monaco - Monte Carlo - 22/05/1966
Total races: 410
Pole positions: 79
Wins: 104
First win: Belgian - Spa - 09/06/1968
Most wins in a season: 15 - 1988
Points: 1915.5
Most points in a season: 199 - 1988
Highest Constructors World Championship position:
Winners 1974, 1984, 1985, 1988, 1989, 1990, 1991
Highest Drivers World Championship position: Winners
1974 (Emerson Fittipaldi), 1976 (James Hunt), 1984 (Niki
Lauda), 1985 (Alain Prost), 1986 (Alain Prost), 1988 (Ayrton
Senna), 1989 (Alain Prost), 1990 (Ayrton Senna), 1991
(Ayrton Senna)

Grand Prix victories: 1968: Bel, It, Can (3) 1969: Mex (1)
1972: SA (1) 1973: Sw, GB, Can (3) 1974: Arg, Bra, Bel,
Can (4) 1975: Arg, Sp, GB (3) 1976: Sp, Fr, Ger, Dut, Can,
US (East) (6) 1977: GB, US (East), Jap (3) 1981: GB (1)
1982: US (West), Bel, Det, GB (4) 1983: US (West) (1)
1984: Bra, SA, SM, Fr, Mon, GB, Ger, Aus, Dut, It, Eur, Por
(12) 1985: Bra, Mon, GB, Aus, Dut, It (6) 1986: SM, Mon,
Aus, Aust (4) 1987: Bra, Bel, Por (3) 1988: Bra, SM, Mon,
Mex, Can, US, Fr, GB, Ger, Hun, Bel, Por, Sp, Jap, Aust (15)
1989: SM, Mon, Mex, US, Fr, GB, Ger, Bel, It, Sp (10) 1990:
US, Mon, Can, Ger, Bel, It (6) 1991: US, Bra, SM, Mon,
Hun, Bel, Jap, Aust (8) 1992: Mon, Can, Hun, It, Aust (5)
1993: Bra, Eur, Mon, Jap, Aust (5)

Constructors Championship 1966-1994: 1966: 9th (2)
1967: 10th (3) 1968: 2nd (49) 1969: 4th (38/40) 1970: =4th
(35) 1971: 6th (10) 1972: 3rd (47/49) 1973: 3rd (58) 1974:
1st (73/75) 1975: 3rd (53) 1976: 2nd (74/75) 1977: 3rd (60)
1978: 8th (15) 1979: 7th (15) 1980: =7th (11) 1981: 6th (28)
1982: 2nd (69) 1983: 5th (34) 1984: 1st (143.5) 1985: 1st
(90) 1986: 2nd (96) 1987: 2nd (76) 1988: 1st (199) 1989: 1st
(141) 1990: 1st (121) 1991: 1st (139) 1992: 2nd (99) 1993:
2nd (84) 1994: 4th (42)

Constructors Championship second team: 1966: 10th (1)
1968: 10th (3)

Martin Brundle crashes out of the Belgium Grand Prix, 1994

MINARDI

Full name: Minardi Scuderia Italia
Address: Minardi Team Spa
Via Spallanzani 21, 48018 Faenza (RA), Italy

Tele: +39 546 620480
Fax: +39 546 620998

Team Principal: Gian Carlo Minardi
Chief Designer: Aldo Costa
Chief Mechanic: Gianluca Gradassi

Engine: Ford HB V8
Chassis: Minardi M194

1994 GRAND PRIX RECORD

Grand Prix	Driver	Pos	Driver	Pos	Pts
1 Brazilian	Alboreto	Ret	Martini	8th	0
2 Pacific	Alboreto	Ret	Martini	Ret	0
3 San Marino	Alboreto	Ret	Martini	Ret	0
4 Monaco	Alboreto	6th	Martini	Ret	1
5 Spanish	Alboreto	Ret	Martini	5th	2
6 Canadian	Alboreto	11th	Martini	9th	0
7 French	Alboreto	Ret	Martini	5th	2
8 British	Alboreto	Ret	Martini	10th	0
9 German	Alboreto	Ret	Martini	Ret	0
10 Hungarian	Alboreto	7th	Martini	Ret	0
11 Belgian	Alboreto	9th	Martini	8th	0
12 Italian	Alboreto	Ret	Martini	Ret	0
13 Portuguese	Alboreto	13th	Martini	12th	0
14 European	Alboreto	14th	Martini	15th	0
15 Japanese	Alboreto	Ret	Martini	20th	0
16 Australian	Alboreto	Ret	Martini	9th	0

Races: 16
Wins: 0
Pole positions: 0
Points: 5
1994 Constructors Championship: 10th

1994 Drivers Championship
Pierluigi Martini: =18th (4)
Michele Alboreto: =24th (1)

COMPLETE GRAND PRIX RECORD
First race: Brazilian - Rio de Janeiro - 07/04/85
Total races: 156
Pole positions: 0
Wins: 0
Highest position: 4th
Top six finishes: 15
Points: 26
Most points in a season: 7 - 1993
Highest Constructors World Championship position: 7th 1991
Highest Drivers World Championship position: 11th 1991 (Pierluigi Martini)

Top six finishes: 1988: US (6) 1989: GB (5/6), Por (5), Aust (6) 1991: SM (4), Por (4) 1992: Jap (6) 1993: SA (4), Eur (6), SM (6), Mon (5) 1994: Mon (6), Sp (5), Fr (5)

Constructors Championship 1985-1994: 1985: - (0) 1986: - (0) 1987: - (0) 1988: 10th (1) 1989: =10th (6) 1990: - (0) 1991: 7th (6) 1992: =11th (1) 1993: 8th (7) 1994: 10th (5)

PACIFIC

Full name: Ursus Pacific Grand Prix Ltd
Address: Pacific Racing Ltd,
Brunel Business Court, Brunel Way, Thetford, Norfolk, IP24
1HP

Tele: +44 (0) 842 755724
Fax: +44 (0)842 755714

Team Principal: Keith Wiggins
Team Manager: Ian Dawson
Chief Mechanic: Jerry Bond

Engine: Ilmor V10
Chassis: Pacific PR01

1994 Test driver: Oliver Gavin

1994 GRAND PRIX RECORD

	Grand Prix	Driver	Pos	Driver	Pos	Pts
1	Brazilian	Belmondo	DNQ	Gachot	Ret	0
2	Pacific	Belmondo	DNQ	Gachot	DNQ	0
3	San Marino	Belmondo	DNQ	Gachot	Ret	0
4	Monaco	Belmondo	Ret	Gachot	Ret	0
5	Spanish	Belmondo	Ret	Gachot	Ret	0
6	Canadian	Belmondo	DNQ	Gachot	Ret	0
7	French	Belmondo	DNQ	Gachot	DNQ	0
8	British	Belmondo	DNQ	Gachot	DNQ	0
9	German	Belmondo	DNQ	Gachot	DNQ	0
10	Hungarian	Belmondo	DNQ	Gachot	DNQ	0
11	Belgian	Belmondo	DNQ	Gachot	DNQ	0
12	Italian	Belmondo	DNQ	Gachot	DNQ	0
13	Portuguese	Belmondo	DNQ	Gachot	DNQ	0
14	European	Belmondo	DNQ	Gachot	DNQ	0
15	Japanese	Belmondo	DNQ	Gachot	DNQ	0
16	Australian	Belmondo	DNQ	Gachot	DNQ	0

Races: 5
Wins: 0
Pole positions: 0
Points: 0
1994 Constructors Championship: No Position

COMPLETE GRAND PRIX RECORD
First race: Brazilian - Interlagos - 27/03/94
Total races: 5
Pole positions: 0
Wins: 0
Highest finish: None
Completed races: 0
Points: 0

Total races: Bra, SM, Mon, Sp, Can

SAUBER

Full name: Sauber Mercedes
Address: PP Sauber AG
Wildbachstrasse 9, CH8340 Hinwil, Switzerland

Tele: +41 (1)938 1400
Fax: +41 (1)938 1670

Team Principal: Peter Sauber
Team Manager/Chief Mechanic: Beat Zehnder
Chief Designer: Leo Ress

Engine: Mercedes Benz V10
Chassis: Sauber C13

1994 GRAND PRIX RECORD

	Grand Prix	Driver	Pos	Driver	Pos	Pts
1	Brazilian	Wendlinger	6th	Frentzen	Ret	1
2	Pacific	Wendlinger	Ret	Frentzen	5th	2
3	San Marino	Wendlinger	4th	Frentzen	7th	3
4	Monaco	Wendlinger	DNR	Frentzen	DNR	0
5	Spanish	No Driver		Frentzen	Ret	0
6	Canadian	de Cesaris	Ret	Frentzen	Ret	0
7	French	de Cesaris	6th	Frentzen	4th	4
8	British	de Cesaris	Ret	Frentzen	7th	0
9	German	de Cesaris	Ret	Frentzen	Ret	0
10	Hungarian	de Cesaris	Ret	Frentzen	Ret	0
11	Belgian	de Cesaris	Ret	Frentzen	Ret	0
12	Italian	de Cesaris	Ret	Frentzen	Ret	0
13	Portuguese	de Cesaris	Ret	Frentzen	Ret	0
14	European	de Cesaris	Ret	Frentzen	6th	1
15	Japanese	Lehto	Ret	Frentzen	6th	1
16	Australian	Lehto	10th	Frentzen	7th	0

Races: 15
Wins: 0
Pole positions: 0
Points: 12
1994 Constructors Championship: 8th

1994 Drivers Championship
Heinz Harald Frentzen: 13th (7)
Karl Wendlinger: =18th (4)
Andrea de Cesaris: =18th* (4)
* Includes 3 points scored in 2 races with Jordan

COMPLETE GRAND PRIX RECORD
First race: South African - Kyalami - 14/03/93
Total races: 31
Pole positions: 0
Wins: 0
Highest finish: 4th
Top six finishes: 13
Points: 24
Most points in a season: 12 - 1993, 1994
Highest Constructors World Championship position:
=6th 1993
Highest Drivers World Championship position: =11th
1993 (Karl Wendlinger)

Top six finishes: 1993: SA (5), SM (4), Can (6), Hun (6), It
(4), Por (5) 1994: Bra (6), Pac (5), SM (4), Fr (4/6), Eur (6),
Jap (6)

Constructors Championship 1993-1994: 1993: =6th (12)
1994: 8th (12)

SIMTEK

Full name: Simtek Ford
Address: Simtek Grand Prix Ltd
8 Wates Ways, Acre Estate, Wildmere Road, Banbury, Oxon,
OX16 7TS

Tele: +44 (0)295 265998
Fax: +44 (0)295 265975

Team Principal: Nicholas Wirth
Team Manager: Charlie Moody
Chief Mechanic: Gary North

Engine: Ford HB V8
Chassis: Simtek S941

1994 GRAND PRIX RECORD

	Grand Prix	Driver	Pos	Driver	Pos	Pts
1	Brazilian	Brabham	12th	Ratzenberger	DNQ	0
2	Pacific	Brabham	Ret	Ratzenberger	11th	0
3	San Marino	Brabham	Ret	Ratzenberger	DNR	0
4	Monaco	Brabham	Ret	No Driver		0
5	Spanish	Brabham	10th	Montermini	DNR	0
6	Canadian	Brabham	14th	No Driver		0
7	French	Brabham	Ret	Gounon	9th	0
8	British	Brabham	15th	Gounon	16th	0
9	German	Brabham	Ret	Gounon	Ret	0
10	Hungarian	Brabham	11th	Gounon	Ret	0
11	Belgian	Brabham	Ret	Gounon	11th	0
12	Italian	Brabham	Ret	Gounon	Ret	0
13	Portuguese	Brabham	Ret	Gounon	15th	0
14	European	Brabham	Ret	Schiattarella	19th	0
15	Japanese	Brabham	12th	Inoue	Ret	0
16	Australian	Brabham	Ret	Schiattarella	Ret	0

Races: 16
Wins: 0
Pole positions: 0
Points: 0
1994 Constructors Championship: No position

COMPLETE GRAND PRIX RECORD
First race: Brazilian - Interlagos - 27/03/94
Total races: 16
Pole positions: 0
Wins: 0
Highest finish: 9th
Completed races: 12
Points: 0

Completed races: 1994: Bra (12), Pac (11), Sp (10), Can (14), Fr (9), GB (15/16), Hun (11), Bel (11), Por (15), Eur (19), Jap (12)

TYRRELL

Full name: Tyrrell Racing Organisation
Address: Tyrrell Racing Organisation Ltd
Long Reach, Ockham, Woking, Surrey, GU23 6PE

Tele: +44 (0)483 284955
Fax: +44 (0)483 284892

Chairman & Team Principal: Ken Tyrrell
Commercial Managing Director: Bob Tyrrell
Technical Managing Director: Dr Harvey Postlethwaite
Team Manager: Rupert Mainwaring
Chief Mechanic: Chris White

Engine: Yamaha OX10A V10
Chassis: Tyrrell 022

1994 GRAND PRIX RECORD

Grand Prix	Driver	Pos	Driver	Pos	Pts
1 Brazilian	Katayama	5th	Blundell	Ret	2
2 Pacific	Katayama	Ret	Blundell	Ret	0
3 San Marino	Katayama	5th	Blundell	9th	2
4 Monaco	Katayama	Ret	Blundell	Ret	0
5 Spanish	Katayama	Ret	Blundell	3rd	4
6 Canadian	Katayama	Ret	Blundell	10th	0
7 French	Katayama	Ret	Blundell	10th	0
8 British	Katayama	6th	Blundell	Ret	1
9 German	Katayama	Ret	Blundell	Ret	0
10 Hungarian	Katayama	Ret	Blundell	5th	2
11 Belgian	Katayama	Ret	Blundell	5th	2
12 Italian	Kayayama	Ret	Blundell	Ret	0
13 Portuguese	Katayama	Ret	Blundell	Ret	0
14 European	Katayama	7th	Blundell	13th	0
15 Japanese	Katayama	Ret	Blundell	Ret	0
16 Australian	Katayama	Ret	Blundell	Ret	0

Races: 16
Wins: 0
Pole positions: 0
Points: 13
1994 Constructors Championship: =6th

1994 Drivers Championship
Mark Blundell: 12th (8)
Ukyo Katayama: 17th (5)

COMPLETE GRAND PRIX RECORD
With Matra-Ford - 1968-69
First race: South African - Kyalami - 01/01/1968
Total races: 23
Pole positions: 2
Wins: 9
First win: Dutch - Zandvoort - 23/06/1968
Points: 111

With March - 1970
First race: South African - Kyalami - 07/03/1970
Total races: 10
Pole positions: 3
Wins: 1
First win: Spanish - Jarama - 19/04/1970
Points: 48

As Tyrrell - 1971-94
First race: Canadian - St Jovite - 20/09/1970
Total races: 364
Pole positions: 14
Wins: 23
First win: Spanish - Montjuich Park - 18/04/1971
Most wins in a season: 7 - 1971
Points: 609
Most points in a season: 86 - 1973

Highest Constructors World Championship position:
Winners 1969 (with Matra-Ford) 1971

Highest Drivers World Championship position: Winners 1969 (Jackie Stewart) (with Matra-Ford), 1971 (Jackie Stewart), 1973 (Jackie Stewart)

Grand Prix victories: (With Matra-Ford) 1968: Dut, Ger, US (3) 1969: SA, Sp, Dut, Fr, GB, It, (6) (With March) 1970: Sp (1) (As Tyrrell) 1971: Sp, Mon, Fr, GB, Ger, Can, US (7) 1972: Arg, Fr, Can, US (4) 1973: SA, Bel, Mon, Dut, Ger (5) 1974: Swe, GB (2) 1975: SA (1) 1976: Swe (1) 1978: Mon (1) 1982: LV (1) 1983: Det (1)

Constructors Championship 1968-1994: (With Matra-Ford) 1968: 3rd (45) 1969: 1st (66) (With March) 1970: 3rd (48) (As Tyrrell) 1970: - (0) 1971: 1st (73) 1972: 2nd (51) 1973: 2nd (82/86) 1974: 3rd (52) 1975: 5th (25) 1976: 3rd (71) 1977: =5th (27) 1978: 4th (38) 1979: 5th (28) 1980: 6th (12) 1981: =8th (10) 1982: 6th (25) 1983: 7th (12) 1984: Dis (0) 1985: 9th (4) 1986: 7th (11) 1987: =6th (11) 1988: 8th (5) 1989: 5th (16) 1990: 5th (16) 1991: 6th (12) 1992: 6th (8) 1993: - (0) 1994: =6th (13)

Constructors Championship second team: 1985: 10th (3)

The Tyrrell's Yamaha Engine

WILLIAMS

Full name: Rothmans Williams Renault
Address: Williams Grand Prix Engineering Ltd
Basil Hill Road, Didcot, Oxon, OX11 7HW

Tele: 44(0) 235 815161
Fax: 44(0) 235 816176

Managing Director: Frank Williams
Technical Director: Patrick Head
Team Manager: Ian Harrison
Chief Designer: Adrian Newey
Chief Mechanic: Dickie Stanford

Engine: Renault V10 RS6
Chassis: Williams FW16

1994 Test Driver: David Coulthard

1994 GRAND PRIX RECORD

	Grand Prix	Driver	Pos	Driver	Pos	Pts
1	Brazilian	Senna	Ret	Hill	2nd	6
2	Pacific	Senna	Ret	Hill	Ret	0
3	San Marino	Senna	Ret	Hill	6th	1
4	Monaco	No Driver	Ret	Hill		0
5	Spanish	Coulthard	Ret	Hill	1st	10
6	Canadian	Coulthard	5th	Hill	2nd	8
7	French	Mansell	Ret	Hill	2nd	6
8	British	Coulthard	5th	Hill	1st	12
9	German	Coulthard	Ret	Hill	8th	0
10	Hungarian	Coulthard	Ret	Hill	2nd	6
11	Belgian	Coulthard	4th	Hill	1st	13
12	Italian	Coulthard	6th	Hill	1st	11
13	Portuguese	Coulthard	2nd	Hill	1st	16
14	European	Mansell	Ret	Hill	2nd	6
15	Japanese	Mansell	4th	Hill	1st	13
16	Australian	Mansell	1st	Hill	Ret	10

Races: 16
Wins: 7
Pole positions: 6
Points: 118
1994 Constructors Championship: Winners

1994 Drivers Championship
Damon Hill: 2nd (91)
David Coulthard: 8th (14)
Nigel Mansell: 9th (13)

COMPLETE GRAND PRIX RECORD
With Brabham 1969, De Tomaso 1970, March 1971-1972
First race: Spanish - Montjuich Park - 04/05/69
Total races: 40
Pole positions: 0
Wins: 0
Highest finish: 2nd
Points: 23

As Williams
First race: Argentine - Buenos Aires - 28/01/73
Total races: 327
Pole positions: 73
Wins: 78
First win: British - Silverstone - 14/07/79
Points: 1456.5
Most wins in a season: 10 - 1992, 1993
Most points in a season: 168 - 1993
Constructors World Championship: Winners 1980, 1981, 1986, 1987, 1992, 1993, 1994
Drivers World Championship: Winners 1980 (Alan Jones), 1982 (Keke Rosberg), 1987 (Nelson Piquet), 1992 (Nigel Mansell), 1993 (Alain Prost)

Grand Prix victories: 1979: GB, Ger, Aus, Dut, Can (5)
1980: Arg, Mon, Fr, GB, Can, US (East) (6) 1981: US
(West), Bra, Bel, LV (4) 1982: Swi (1) 1983: Mon (1) 1984
Dal (1) 1985: Det, Eur, SA, Aust (4) 1986: Bra, Bel, Can, Fr,

GB, Ger, Hun, It, Por (9) 1987: SM, Fr, GB, Ger, Hun, Aus, It, Sp, Mex (9) 1989: Can, Aust (2) 1990: SM, Hun (2) 1991: Mex, Fr, GB, Ger, It, Por, Sp (7) 1992: SA, Mex, Bra, Sp, SM, Fr, GB, Ger, Por, Jap (10) 1993: SA, SM, Sp, Can, Fr, GB, Ger, Hun, Bel, It (10) 1994: Sp, GB, Bel, It, Por, Jap, Aust (7)

Constructors Championship 1972-1994: (With Brabham) 1969: - (16) (With De Tomaso) 1970: - (0) (With March) 1971: - (4) 1972: - (3) (As Williams) 1973: 10th (2) 1974: 10th (4) 1975: 9th (6) 1976: - (0) (As Williams GP Engineering) 1977: - (0) 1978: =9th (11) 1979: 2nd (75), 1980: 1st (120) 1981: 1st (95) 1982: 4th (58) 1983: 4th (36) 1984: 6th (25.5) 1985: =3rd (71) 1986: 1st (141) 1987: 1st (137) 1988: 7th (20) 1989: 2nd (77) 1990: 4th (57) 1991: 2nd (125) 1992: 1st (108) 1993: 1st (168) 1994: 1st (118)

Constructors Championship second team: 1983: 11th (2)

Damon Hill with some of the Williams team

The Williams team at work

Circuits

Monaco   where else!

INTERLAGOS

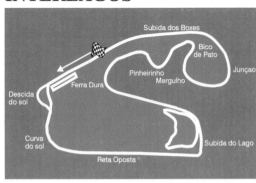

CIRCUIT DETAILS

Name: Autodromo Jose Carlos Pace
Address: Avenida senador Teotonio
Vilela 261
Sao Paulo, Brazil

Tele: (55) 21 5219911/5219832
Fax: (55) 21 2473766

Lap distance: 4.325kms
Laps per race: 71
Full race distance: 307.075kms
Lap record: Michael Schumacher - 1'18.455 - 27/03/94

1994 Race
Winner: Michael Schumacher - Benetton-Ford
Pole position: Ayrton Senna - 1'15.962
Fastest lap: Michael Schumacher - 1'18.455

Races: 12
First race: 11/02/1973
Winner: Emerson Fittipaldi
Most wins (driver): Emerson Fittipaldi (2), Ayrton Senna (2)
Most wins (constructor): Ferrari (3), McLaren (3)

AIDA

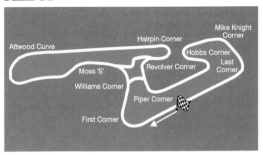

CIRCUIT DETAILS

Name: TI Circuit AIDA
Address: Yasutaka Kawashima
1210 Takimiya, Aida-cho
Okayama 701-25, Japan

Tele: (81) 8687-4-3311
Fax: (81) 8687-4-2600

Lap distance: 3.703kms
Laps per race: 83
Full race distance: 307.339kms
Lap record: 1'14.023 - Michael Schumacher - 17/04/94

1994 Race
Winner: Michael Schumacher - Benetton-Ford
Pole position: Ayrton Senna - 1'10.218
Fastest lap: Michael Schumacher - 1'14.023

IMOLA

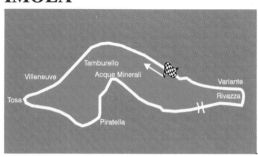

CIRCUIT DETAILS

Name: Autodromo Enzo y Dino Ferrari
Address: Viale Dante, 40026 Imola, San Marino

Tele: (39) 542 31444
Fax: (39) 542 30420

Lap distance: 5.040kms
Laps per race: 61
Full race distance: 307.44kms
Lap record: 1'24.335 - Damon Hill - 01/05/94

1994 Race
Winner: Michael Schumacher - Benetton-Ford
Pole position: Ayrton Senna - 1'21.548
Fastest lap: Damon Hill - 1'24.335

Races: 15*
First race: 03/05/1981
Winner: Nelson Piquet
Most wins (driver): Alain Prost (3), Ayrton Senna (3)
Most wins (constructor): McLaren (5), Williams (4)

* Including the 1980 Italian Grand Prix

MONACO

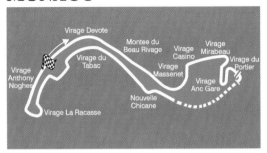

CIRCUIT DETAILS

Name: Circuit de Monaco
Address: Automobile Club de Monaco
23 Boulevard Albert 1er
BP 464, Monaco

Tele: (33) 93152600
Fax: (33) 93258008

Lap distance: 3.328kms
Laps per race: 78
Full race distance: 259.584kms
Lap record: 1:21.078 - Michael Schumacher - 15/05/94

1994 Race
Winner: Michael Schumacher - Benetton-Ford
Pole position: Michael Schumacher - 1'18.560
Fastest lap: Michael Schumacher - 1'21.076

Races: 41
First race: 21/05/1950
Winner: Juan Manuel Fangio
Most wins (driver): Ayrton Senna (6), Graham Hill (5),
Alain Prost (4)
Most wins (constructor): McLaren (9), Lotus (7)

BARCELONA

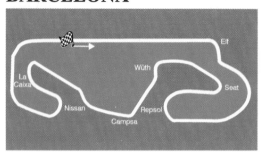

CIRCUIT DETAILS

Name: Circuit de Catalunya
Address: Km2, Carretera de Granollers
Montmelo
Barcelona, Spain

Tele: (34) 3 5719700/5721681
Fax: (34) 3 5723061

Lap distance: 4.747kms
Laps per race: 65
Full race distance: 308.555kms
Lap record: 1'20.989 - Michael Schumacher - 09/05/93

1994 Race
Winner: Damon Hill - Williams-Renault
Pole position: 1'21.908 - Michael Schumacher
Fastest lap: 1'25.155 - Michael Schumacher

Races: 4
First race: 29/09/1991
Winner: Nigel Mansell
Most wins (driver): Nigel Mansell (2)
Most wins (constructor): Williams (4)

MONTREAL

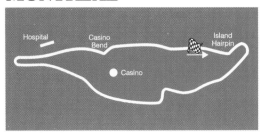

CIRCUIT DETAILS

Name: Circuit Gilles Villeneuve
Address: Grand Prix du Canada
Bassin Olympique
Ile Notre Dame
Montreal, Quebec H3C 1AO, Canada

Tele: (1) 514 3924731
Fax: (1) 514 3920007

Lap distance: 4.430kms
Laps per race: 69
Full race distance: 305.670kms
Lap record: 1'19.775 - Ayrton Senna - 14/06/92

1994 Race
Winner: Michael Schumacher - Benetton-Ford
Pole position: 1'26.178 - Michael Schumacher
Fastest lap: 1'28.927 - Michael Schumacher

Races: 16
First race: 08/10/1978
Winner: Gilles Villeneuve
Most wins (driver): Nelson Piquet (3)
Most wins (constructor): Williams (5)

MAGNY-COURS

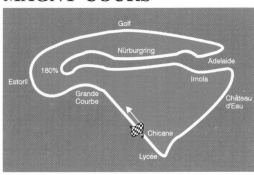

CIRCUIT DETAILS

Name: Circuit de Nevers Magny-Cours
Address: Technopole
58470 Magny-Cours
France

Tele: (33) 86218000
Fax: (33) 86218080

Lap distance: 4.25kms
Laps per race: 72
Full race distance: 306kms
Lap record: 1'17.070 - Nigel Mansell - 05/07/92

1994 Race
Winner: Michael Schumacher - Benetton-Ford
Pole position: Damon Hill - 1'16.282
Fastest lap: Damon Hill - 1'19.678

Races: 4
First race: 07/07/1991
Winner: Nigel Mansell
Most wins (driver): Nigel Mansell (2)
Most wins (constructor): Williams (3)

SILVERSTONE

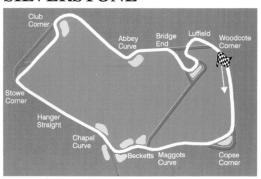

CIRCUIT DETAILS

Name: Silverstone
Address: Silverstone Circuits Limited
Silverstone, near Towcester,
Northamptonshire, NN12 8TN, Great Britain

Tele: (0327) 857271
Fax: (0327) 857663

Lap distance: 5.226kms
Laps per race: 59
Full race distance: 308.334kms
Lap record: 1'22.515 - Damon Hill - 11/07/93

After 1994 modifications
Lap distance: 5.16kms
Laps per race: 60
Full race distance: 309.60kms

1994 Race
Winner: Damon Hill - Williams-Renault
Pole position: Damon Hill - 1'24.960
Fastest lap: Damon Hill - 1'27.100

Races: 28
First race: 13/05/1950
Winner: Giuseppe Farina
Most wins (driver): Alain Prost (5), Jim Clark (3), Nigel
Mansell (3)
Most wins (constructor): Ferrari (7), McLaren (7),
Williams (6)

HOCKENHEIM

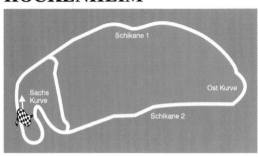

CIRCUIT DETAILS

Name: Hockenmeimring
Address: Postfach 1106
6832 Hockenheim
Germany

Tele: (49) 6205 9500
Fax: (49) 6205 950299

Lap distance: 6.815kms
Laps per race: 45
Full race distance: 306.675kms
Lap record: 1'41.591 - Riccardo Patrese - 26/07/92

After 1994 modifications
Lap distance: 6.823kms
Laps per race: 45
Full race distance: 307.035kms

1994 Race
Winner: Gerhard Berger - Ferrari
Pole position: Gerhard Berger - 1'43.582
Fastest lap: David Coulthard - 1'46.211

Races: 18
First race: 02/08/1970
Winner: Jochen Rindt
Most wins (driver): Nelson Piquet (3), Ayrton Senna (3),
Alain Prost (2), Nigel Mansell (2)
Most wins (constructor): Williams (6), Ferrari (4),
McLaren (4)

HUNGARORING

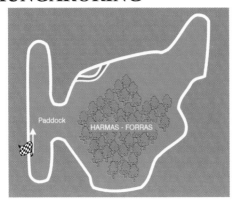

CIRCUIT DETAILS

Name: Hungaroring
Address: PF10, 2146 Mogyorod
Hungary
Tele: (36) 628 330040

Lap distance: 3.968kms
Laps per race: 77
Full race distance: 305.536kms
Lap record: 1'18.308 - Nigel Mansell - 16/08/92

1994 Race
Winner: Michael Schumacher - Benetton-Ford
Pole position: 1'18.258 - Michael Schumacher
Fastest lap: 1'20.881 - Michael Schumacher

Races: 9
First race: 10/08/1986
Winner: Nelson Piquet
Most wins (driver): Ayrton Senna (3), Nelson Piquet (2)
Most wins (constructor): Williams (4), McLaren (3)

SPA FRANCORCHAMPS

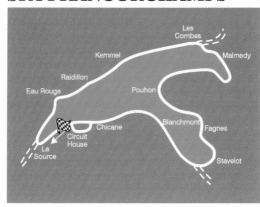

CIRCUIT DETAILS

Name: Circuit de Spa Francorchamps
Address: Circuit House
Route du Circuit 55
4970 Francorchamps
Belgium

Tele: (32) 87 275138
Fax: (32) 87 275296

Lap distance: 6.974kms
Laps per race: 44
Full race distance: 306.865kms
Lap record: 1'51.095 - Alain Prost - 29/09/93

1994 Race
Winner: Damon Hill - Williams-Renault
Pole Position: 2'21.163 - Rubens Barrichello
Fastest lap: 1'57.117 - Damon Hill

Races: 29
First race: 18/06/1950
Winner: Juan Manuel Fangio
Most wins (driver): Ayrton Senna (5), Jim Clark (4), Juan Manuel Fangio (3)
Most wins (constructor): McLaren (6), Ferrari (5), Lotus (5)

MONZA

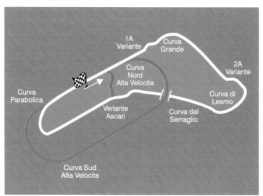

CIRCUIT DETAILS

Name: Autodromo Nationale di Monza
Address: Parco Monza
20052 Monza
Italy

Tele: (39) 39 24821
Fax: (39) 39 320324

Lap distance: 5.80kms
Laps per race: 53
Full race distance: 307.40kms
Lap record: 1'23.575 - Damon Hill - 12/09/93

1994 Race
Winner: Damon Hill - Williams-Renault
Pole position: 1'23.844 - Jean Alesi
Fastest lap: 1'25.930 - Damon Hill

Races: 44
First race: 03/09/1950
Winner: Giuseppe Farina
Most wins (driver): Juan Manuel Fangio (3), Stirling Moss (3), Ronnie Peterson (3), Nelson Piquet (3), Alain Prost (3)
Most wins (constructor): Ferrari (10)

ESTORIL

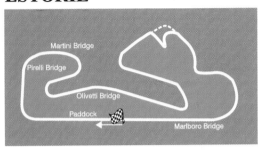

CIRCUIT DETAILS

Name: Autodromo de Estoril
Address: Km 6, Estrada Nacional 9
Alcabideche, 2765 Estoril
Portugal

Tele: (351) 1 4691462
Fax: (351) 1 4691202

Lap distance: 4.35kms
Laps per race: 71
Full race distance: 308.85kms
Lap record: 1'14.859 - Damon Hill - 26/09/93

1994 Race
Winner: Damon Hill - Williams-Renault
Pole position: 1'20.608 - Gerhard Berger
Fastest lap: 1'22.446 - David Coulthard

Races: 11
First race: 21/10/1984
Winner: Alain Prost
Most wins (driver): Alain Prost (3), Nigel Mansell (3)
Most wins (constructor): Williams (4), McLaren (3)

JEREZ

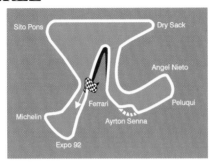

CIRCUIT DETAILS

Name: Circuit de Jerez
Address: Carretera Jerez Km 10
Apartado de Correos 1709
Jerez de la Frontera
Cadiz, Spain

Tele: (34) 5615 1100
Fax: (34) 5615 1105

Lap distance: 4.423kms
Laps per race: 70
Full race distance: 309.61kms
Lap record: 1'24.513 - Riccardo Patrese - 30/09/90

After 1994 modifications
Lap distance: 4.428kms
Laps per race: 69
Full race distance: 305.532kms

1994 Race
Winner: Michael Schumacher - Benetton-Ford
Pole position: Michael Schumacher - 1'22.762
Fastest lap: Michael Schumacher - 1'25.040

Races: 6*
First race: 25/09/1983
Winner: Nelson Piquet
Most wins (driver): Ayrton Senna (2), Alain Prost (2)
Most wins (constructor): McLaren (2)

* Including the 1994 European Grand Prix

SUZUKA

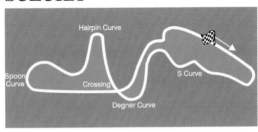

CIRCUIT DETAILS

Name: Suzuka International Racing Course
Address: 7992 Ino-Cho
Suzuka-Shi
Mie-Ken 510-02
Japan

Tele: (81) 573 781111
Fax: (81) 593 70 1818

Lap distance: 5.864kms
Laps per race: 53
Full race distance: 310.792kms
Lap record: 1'40.646 - Nigel Mansell - 25/10/92

1994 Race
Winner: Damon Hill - Williams-Renault
Pole position: Michael Schumacher - 1'37.209
Fastest lap: Damon Hill - 1'56.597

Races: 8
First race: 01/11/1987
Winner: Gerhard Berger
Most wins (driver): Gerhard Berger (2), Ayrton Senna (2)
Most wins (constructor): McLaren (4)

ADELAIDE

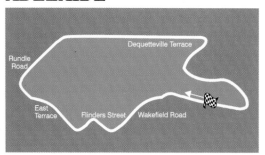

CIRCUIT DETAILS

Name: Adelaide Grand Prix Circuit
Address: Australian Formula 1 Grand Prix Office
300 Rundle Street, 1st Floor
Adelaide 5000 South Australia
Australia

Tele: (61) 8 2231111
Fax: (61) 8 2324144

Lap distance: 3.780kms
Laps per race: 81
Full race distance: 306.18kms
Lap record: 1'15.381 - Damon Hill - 07/11/93

1994 Race
Winner: Nigel Mansell - Williams-Renault
Pole position: Nigel Mansell - 1'16.179
Fastest lap: Nigel Mansell - 1'17.140

Races: 10
First race: 03/11/1985
Winner: Keke Rosberg
Most wins (driver): Alain Prost (2), Gerhard Berger (2),
Ayrton Senna (2)
Most wins (constructor): McLaren (5), Williams (3)

Nigel Mansell wins the Australian Grand Prix 1994

Driver Profiles

Formula One drivers 1994

MICHELE ALBORETO

Born: 23/12/56   **Country:** Italy

Grand Prix debut: San Marino - Imola - 03/05/81
Starts: 194   **Wins:** 5
First win: Las Vegas - Caesar's Palace - 25/09/82
Pole positions: 2   **Top six finishes:** 47
Points: 186.5
Highest World Championship position: 2nd 1985
Racing teams: Tyrrell 81-83, Ferrari 84-88, Tyrrell 89,
Larrousse 89, Footwork 90-92, Lola 93, Minardi 94

COMPLETE GRAND PRIX CAREER RECORD

	GP	1st	2nd	3rd	4th	5th	6th	OFP	RET	DIS	PTS	WCP
1981	10	0	0	0	0	0	0	4	6	0	0	-
1982	16	1	0	1	3	1	1	4	5	0	25	7=
1983	15	1	0	0	0	0	1	5	8	0	10	12=
1984	16	1	2	1	1	1	1	1	8	0	30.5	4
1985	16	2	4	2	1	0	0	1	6	0	53	2
1986	16	0	1	0	2	1	0	3	9	0	14	8=
1987	16	0	1	2	1	0	0	1	11	0	17	7
1988	16	0	1	2	2	2	0	3	6	0	24	5
1989	10	0	0	1	0	1	0	2	6	0	6	11=
1990	13	0	0	0	0	0	0	8	5	0	0	-
1991	9	0	0	0	0	0	0	2	7	0	0	-
1992	16	0	0	0	0	2	2	10	2	0	6	10
1993	9	0	0	0	0	0	0	4	5	0	0	-
1994	16	0	0	0	0	0	1	5	10	0	1	24=
Total	194	5	9	9	10	8	6	53	94	0	186.5	

Grand Prix victories: 1982: LV   1983: Det 1984: Bel 1985:
Can, Ger

JEAN ALESI

Born: 11/06/64   **Country:** France

Grand Prix debut: French - Paul Ricard - 09/07/89
Starts: 85   **Wins:** 0
Highest finish: 2nd
Pole positions: 1   **Top six finishes:** 30
Points: 100
Highest World Championship position: 5th 1994
Racing teams: Tyrrell 89-90, Ferrari 91-94

COMPLETE GRAND PRIX CAREER RECORD

	GP	1st	2nd	3rd	4th	5th	6th	OFP	RET	DIS	PTS	WCP
1989	8	0	0	0	2	1	0	2	3	0	8	9
1990	15	0	2	0	0	0	1	6	6	0	13	9
1991	16	0	0	3	2	1	1	1	8	0	21	7
1992	16	0	0	2	2	2	0	0	10	0	18	7
1993	16	0	1	1	2	0	0	3	9	0	16	6
1994	14	0	1	3	1	1	1	1	6	0	24	5
Total	**85**	**0**	**4**	**9**	**9**	**5**	**3**	**13**	**42**	**0**	**100**	

Top six finishes: 1989: Fr (4), It (5), Sp (4) 1990: US (2),
SM (6), Mon (2) 1991: Bra (6), Mon (3), Fr (4), Ger (3), Hun
(5), Por (3), Sp (4) 1992: Bra (4), Sp (3), Can (3), Ger (5),
Jap (5), Aust (4) 1993: Mon (3), It (2), Por (4), Aust (4)
1994: Bra (3), Mon (5), Sp (4), Can (3), GB (2), Jap (3), Aust
(6)

PHILIPPE ALLIOT

Born: 27/07/54   **Country:** France

Grand Prix debut: Brazilian - Rio de Janeiro - 25/03/84
Starts: 109   **Wins:** 0
Highest finish: 5th
Pole positions: 0   **Top six finishes:** 6
Points: 7
Highest World Championship position: =16th 1987
Racing teams: RAM 84-85, Ligier 86, Larrousse 87-89, Ligier 90, Larrousse 93-94, McLaren 94, Larrousse 94

COMPLETE GRAND PRIX CAREER RECORD

	GP	1st	2nd	3rd	4th	5th	6th	OFP	RET	DIS	PTS	WCP
1984	13	0	0	0	0	0	0	3	10	0	0	-
1985	13	0	0	0	0	0	0	1	12	0	0	-
1986	7	0	0	0	0	0	1	2	4	0	1	18=
1987	15	0	0	0	0	0	3	3	9	0	3	16=
1988	16	0	0	0	0	0	0	8	8	0	0	-
1989	15	0	0	0	0	0	1	3	11	0	1	26=
1990	14	0	0	0	0	0	0	9	4	1	0	-
1993	14	0	0	0	0	1	0	9	4	0	2	17=
1994	2	0	0	0	0	0	0	0	2	0	0	-
Total	**109**	**0**	**0**	**0**	**0**	**1**	**5**	**38**	**64**	**1**	**7**	

Top six finishes: 1986: Mex (6) 1987: Ger (6), Sp (6), Mex (6) 1989: Sp (6) 1993: SM (5)

RUBENS BARRICHELLO

Born: 23/05/72   **Country:** Brazil

Grand Prix debut: South African - Kyalami - 14/03/93
Starts: 31   **Wins:** 0
Highest finish: 3rd
Pole positions: 1   **Top six finishes:** 7
Points: 21
Highest World Championship position: 6th 1994
Racing teams: Jordan 93-94

COMPLETE GRAND PRIX CAREER RECORD

	GP	1st	2nd	3rd	4th	5th	6th	OFP	RET	DIS	PTS	WCP
1993	16	0	0	0	0	1	0	7	8	0	2	17=
1994	15	0	0	1	5	0	0	2	7	0	19	6
Total	**31**	**0**	**0**	**1**	**5**	**1**	**0**	**9**	**15**	**0**	**21**	

Top six finishes: 1993: Jap (5) 1994: Bra (4), Pac (3), GB (4), It (4), Por (4), Aust (4)

PAUL BELMONDO

Born: 23/04/63   **Country:** France

Grand Prix debut: Spanish - Barcelona - 03/05/92
Starts: 7   **Wins:** 0
Highest finish: 9th
Pole positions: 0
Completed races: 5
Points: 0
Highest World Championship position: None
Racing teams: March 92, Pacific 94

COMPLETE GRAND PRIX CAREER RECORD

	GP	1st	2nd	3rd	4th	5th	6th	OFP	RET	DIS	PTS	WCP
1992	5	0	0	0	0	0	0	5	0	0	0	-
1994	2	0	0	0	0	0	0	0	2	0	0	-
Total	**7**	**0**	**0**	**0**	**0**	**0**	**0**	**5**	**2**	**0**	**0**	

Highest race positions: 1992: Sp (12), SM (13), Can (14), Ger (13), Hun (9)

OLIVER BERETTA

Born: 23/11/69   **Country:** France

Grand Prix debut: Brazilian - Interlagos - 27/03/94
Starts: 10   **Wins:** 0
Highest finish: 7th
Pole positions: 0
Completed races: 4
Points: 0
Highest World Championship position: None
Racing teams: Larrousse 94

COMPLETE GRAND PRIX CAREER RECORD

	GP	1st	2nd	3rd	4th	5th	6th	OFP	RET	DIS	PTS	WCP
1994	10	0	0	0	0	0	0	4	6	0	0	-
Total	10	0	0	0	0	0	0	4	6	0	0	-

Highest race positions: 1994: Mon (8), GB (14), Ger (7), Hun (9)

GERHARD BERGER

Born: 27/08/59   **Country:** Austria

Grand Prix debut: Austrian - Osterreichring - 19/08/84
Starts: 163   **Wins:** 9
First win: Mexican - Mexico City - 12/10/86
Pole positions: 10   **Top six finishes:** 72
Points: 306
Highest World Championship position: 3rd 1988, 1994
Racing teams: Team ATS 84, Arrows 85, Benetton 86,
Ferrari 87-89, McLaren 90-92, Ferrari 93-94

COMPLETE GRAND PRIX CAREER RECORD

	GP	1st	2nd	3rd	4th	5th	6th	OFP	RET	DIS	PTS	WCP
1984	4	0	0	0	0	0	1*	2	1	0	0	-
1985	16	0	0	0	0	1	1	7	7	0	3	17=
1986	16	1	0	1	0	1	2	3	8	0	17	7
1987	16	2	1	0	4	0	0	0	9	0	36	5
1988	16	1	2	2	3	1	1	1	5	0	41	3
1989	15	1	2	0	0	0	0	0	12	0	21	7
1990	16	0	2	5	3	1	0	2	3	0	43	4
1991	16	1	3	2	3	0	0	0	7	0	43	4
1992	16	2	2	1	3	2	0	0	6	0	49	5
1993	16	0	0	1	1	1	3	3	7	0	12	8
1994	16	1	3	2	1	1	0	1	7	0	41	3
Total	163	9	15	14	18	8	8	19	72	0	306	

Grand Prix victories: 1986: Mex 1987: Jap, Aust 1988: It
1989: Por 1991: Jap 1992: Can, Aust 1994: Ger
* Ineligible for points

ERIC BERNARD

Born: 24/08/64   **Country:** France

Grand Prix debut: French - Paul Ricard - 09/07/89
Starts: 45   **Wins:** 0
Highest finish: 3rd
Pole positions: 0   **Top six finishes:** 5
Points: 10
Highest World Championship position: 13th 1990
Racing teams: Larrousse 89-91, Ligier 94, Lotus 94

COMPLETE GRAND PRIX CAREER RECORD

	GP	1st	2nd	3rd	4th	5th	6th	OFP	RET	DIS	PTS	WCP
1989	2	0	0	0	0	0	0	1	1	0	0	-
1990	16	0	0	0	1	0	2	5	8	0	5	13
1991	13	0	0	0	0	0	1	1	11	0	1	18=
1994	14	0	0	1	0	0	0	10	3	0	4	18=
Total	45	0	0	1	1	0	3	17	23	0	10	

Top six finishes: 1990: Mon (6), GB (4), Hun (6) 1991: Mex (6) 1994: Ger (3)

MARK BLUNDELL

Born: 08/04/66   **Country:** Great Britain

Grand Prix debut: United States - Phoenix - 10/03/91
Starts: 46   **Wins:** 0
Highest finish: 3rd
Pole positions: 0   **Top six finishes:** 7
Points: 19
Highest World Championship position: 10th 1993
Racing teams: Brabham 91, Ligier 93, Tyrrell 94

COMPLETE GRAND PRIX CAREER RECORD

	GP	1st	2nd	3rd	4th	5th	6th	OFP	RET	DIS	PTS	WCP
1991	14	0	0	0	0	0	1	4	9	0	1	18=
1993	16	0	0	2	0	1	0	6	7	0	10	10
1994	16	0	0	1	0	2	0	4	9	0	8	12
Total	**46**	**0**	**0**	**3**	**0**	**3**	**1**	**14**	**25**	**0**	**19**	

Top six finishes: 1991: Bel (6) 1993: SA (3), Bra (5), Ger (3) 1994: Sp (3), Hun (5), Bel (5)

THIERRY BOUTSEN

Born: 13/07/57   **Country:** Belgium

Grand Prix debut: Belgian - Spa - 22/05/83
Starts: 163   **Wins:** 3
First win: Canadian - Montreal - 18/06/89
Pole positions: 1   **Top six finishes:** 41
Points: 132
Highest World Championship position: 4th 1988
Racing teams: Arrows 83-86, Benetton 87-88, Williams 89-90, Ligier 91-92, Jordan 93

COMPLETE GRAND PRIX CAREER RECORD

	GP	1st	2nd	3rd	4th	5th	6th	OFP	RET	DIS	PTS	WCP
1983	10	0	0	0	0	0	0	8	2	0	0	-
1984	15	0	0	0	0	2	1	4	8	0	5	14=
1985	16	0	1	0	1	0	2	8	4	0	11	11
1986	16	0	0	0	0	0	0	6	10	0	0	-
1987	16	0	0	1	2	3	0	3	7	0	16	8
1988	16	0	0	5	1	1	2	4	2	1	27	4
1989	16	2	0	3	2	0	1	2	6	0	37	5
1990	16	1	1	1	2	4	1	0	6	0	34	6
1991	16	0	0	0	0	0	0	10	6	0	0	-
1992	16	0	0	0	0	1	0	6	9	0	2	14=
1993	10	0	0	0	0	0	0	5	5	0	0	-
Total	**163**	**3**	**2**	**10**	**8**	**11**	**7**	**56**	**65**	**1**	**132**	

Grand Prix victories: 1989: Can, Aust 1990: Hun

DAVID BRABHAM

Born: 05/09/65　　　　**Country:** Australia

Grand Prix debut: Monaco - Monte Carlo - 27/05/90
Starts: 24　　　　**Wins:** 0
Highest finish: 10th
Pole positions: 0
Completed races: 7
Points: 0
Highest World Championship position: None
Racing teams: Brabham 90, Simtek 94

COMPLETE GRAND PRIX CAREER RECORD

	GP	1st	2nd	3rd	4th	5th	6th	OFP	RET	DIS	PTS	WCP
1990	8	0	0	0	0	0	0	1	7	0	0	-
1994	16	0	0	0	0	0	0	6	10	0	0	-
Total	24	0	0	0	0	0	0	7	17	0	0	

Highest race positions: 1990: Fr (15) 1994: Bra (12), Sp (10), Can (14), GB (15), Hun (11), Jap (12)

MARTIN BRUNDLE

Born: 01/06/59   **Country:** Great Britain

Grand Prix debut: Brazilian - Rio de Janeiro - 25/03/84
Starts: 131   **Wins:** 0
Highest finish: 2nd
Pole positions: 0   **Top six finishes:** 32
Points: 83
Highest World Championship position: 6th 1992
Racing teams: Tyrrell 84-86, Zakspeed 87, Williams 88,
Brabham 89, 91, Benetton 92, Ligier 93, McLaren 94

COMPLETE GRAND PRIX CAREER RECORD

	GP	1st	2nd	3rd	4th	5th	6th	OFP	RET	DIS	PTS	WCP
1984	7	0	0	0	0	0	0	0	0	7	0	-
1985	15	0	0	0	0	0	0	10	5	0	0	-
1986	16	0	0	0	1	2	1	5	7	0	8	11
1987	16	0	0	0	0	1	0	2	12	1	2	18
1988	1	0	0	0	0	0	0	1	0	0	0	-
1989	14	0	0	0	0	1	2	4	7	0	4	16=
1991	14	0	0	0	0	1	0	8	5	0	2	15=
1992	16	0	1	4	4	2	0	0	5	0	38	6
1993	16	0	0	1	0	3	3	4	5	0	13	7
1994	16	0	1	1	1	1	1	1	10	0	16	7
Total	**131**	**0**	**2**	**6**	**6**	**11**	**7**	**35**	**56**	**8**	**83**	

Top six finishes: 1986: Bra (5), GB (5), Hun (6), Aust (4)
1987: SM (5) 1989: Mon (6), It (6), Jap (5) 1991: Jap (5)
1992: SM (4), Mon (5), Fr (3), GB (3), Ger (4), Hun (5), Bel
(4), It (2), Por (4), Jap (3), Aust (3) 1993: SM (3), Mon (6),
Can (5), Fr (5), Hun (5), Por (6), Aust (6) 1994: Mon (2),
Hun (4), It (5), Por (6), Aust (3)

ANDREA DE CESARIS

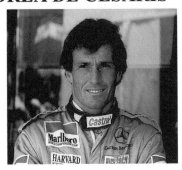

Born: 31/05/59   **Country:** Italy

Grand Prix debut: Canadian - Montreal - 28/09/80

Starts: 208   **Wins:** 0

Highest finish: 2nd

Pole positions: 1   **Top six finishes:** 22

Points: 59

Highest World Championship position: 8th 1983

Racing teams: Alfa Romeo 80, McLaren 81, Alfa Romeo 82-83, Ligier 84-85, Minardi 86, Brabham 87, Rial 88, Dallara 89-90, Jordan 91, Tyrrell 92-93, Jordan 94, Sauber 94

COMPLETE GRAND PRIX CAREER RECORD

	GP	1st	2nd	3rd	4th	5th	6th	OFP	RET	DIS	PTS	WCP
1980	2	0	0	0	0	0	0	0	2	0	0	-
1981	14	0	0	0	0	0	1	5	8	0	1	18=
1982	16	0	0	1	0	0	1	4	10	0	5	17=
1983	14	0	2	0	1	0	0	2	9	0	15	8
1984	16	0	0	0	0	1	1	5	9	0	3	16=
1985	11	0	0	0	1	0	0	2	8	0	3	17=
1986	15	0	0	0	0	0	0	1	14	0	0	-
1987	16	0	0	1	0	0	0	1	14	0	4	14=
1988	16	0	0	0	1	0	0	4	11	0	3	15
1989	15	0	0	1	0	0	0	7	7	0	4	16=
1990	15	0	0	0	0	0	0	2	12	1	0	-
1991	15	0	0	0	2	1	1	5	6	0	9	9
1992	16	0	0	0	1	2	1	4	8	0	8	9
1993	16	0	0	0	0	0	0	5	10	1	0	-
1994	11	0	0	0	1	0	1	0	9	0	4	18=
Total	**208**	**0**	**2**	**3**	**7**	**4**	**6**	**47**	**137**	**2**	**59**	

Top six finishes: 1981: SM (6) 1982: Mon (3), Can (6) 1983: Ger (2), Eur (4), SA (2) 1984: SA (5), SM (6) 1985: Mon (4) 1987: Bel (3) 1988: US (4) 1989: Can (3) 1991: Can (4), Mex (4), Fr (6), Ger (5) 1992: Mex (5), Can (5), It (6), Jap (4) 1994: Mon (4), Fr (6)

ERIK COMAS

Born: 28/09/63   **Country:** France

Grand Prix debut: Brazilian - Interlagos - 24/03/91
Starts: 59   **Wins:** 0
Highest finish: 5th
Pole positions: 0   **Top six finishes:** 6
Points: 7
Highest World Championship position: 11th 1992
Racing teams: Ligier 91-92, Larrousse 93-94

COMPLETE GRAND PRIX CAREER RECORD

	GP	1st	2nd	3rd	4th	5th	6th	OFP	RET	DIS	PTS	WCP
1991	13	0	0	0	0	0	0	8	5	0	0	-
1992	15	0	0	0	0	1	2	4	8	0	4	11
1993	16	0	0	0	0	0	1	7	8	0	1	20=
1994	15	0	0	0	0	0	2	5	8	0	2	23
Total	**59**	**0**	**0**	**0**	**0**	**1**	**5**	**24**	**29**	**0**	**7**	

Top six finishes: 1992: Can (6), Fr (5), Ger (6) 1993: It (6)
1994: Pac (6), Ger (6)

DAVID COULTHARD

Born: 27/03/71   **Country:** Great Britain

Grand Prix debut: Spanish - Barcelona - 29/05/94
Starts: 8   **Wins:** 0
Highest finish: 2nd
Pole positions: 0   **Top six finishes:** 5
Points: 14
Highest World Championship position: 8th 1994
Racing teams: Williams 94

COMPLETE GRAND PRIX CAREER RECORD

	GP	1st	2nd	3rd	4th	5th	6th	OFP	RET	DIS	PTS	WCP
1994	8	0	1	0	1	2	1	0	3	0	14	8
Total	8	0	1	0	1	2	1	0	3	0	14	8

Top six finishes: Can (5), GB (5), Bel (4), It (6), Por (2)

YANNICK DALMAS

Born: 28/07/61   **Country:** France

Grand Prix debut: Mexican - Mexico City - 18/10/87
Starts: 24   **Wins:** 0
Highest finish: 5th
Pole positions: 0   **Top six finishes:** 1
Points: 0
Highest World Championship position: None
Racing teams: Minardi 93, Simtek 94

COMPLETE GRAND PRIX CAREER RECORD

	GP	1st	2nd	3rd	4th	5th	6th	OFP	RET	DIS	PTS	WCP
1987	3	0	0	0	0	1*	0	2	0	0	0	-
1988	13	0	0	0	0	0	0	8	5	0	0	-
1989	1	0	0	0	0	0	0	0	1	0	0	-
1990	5	0	0	0	0	0	0	3	2	0	0	-
1994	2	0	0	0	0	0	0	1	1	0	0	-
Total	24	0	0	0	0	1	0	14	9	0	0	

Top six finishes: 1987: Aust (5)
* Not entered in Championship, ineligible for points

CHRISTIAN FITTIPALDI

Born: 18/01/71   **Country:** Brazil

Grand Prix debut: South African - Kyalami - 01/03/92
Starts: 40   **Wins:** 0
Highest finish: 4th
Pole positions: 0   **Top six finishes:** 5
Points: 12
Highest World Championship position: =13th 1993
Racing teams: Minardi 92-93, Arrows 94

COMPLETE GRAND PRIX CAREER RECORD

	GP	1st	2nd	3rd	4th	5th	6th	OFP	RET	DIS	PTS	WCP
1992	10	0	0	0	0	0	1	5	4	0	1	17=
1993	14	0	0	0	1	1	0	8	4	0	5	13=
1994	16	0	0	0	2	0	0	7	6	1	6	14=
Total	**40**	**0**	**0**	**0**	**3**	**1**	**1**	**20**	**14**	**1**	**12**	

Top six finishes: 1992: Jap (6) 1993: SA (4), Mon (5) 1994: Pac (4), Ger (4)

HEINZ-HARALD FRENTZEN

Born: 18/05/67   **Country:** Germany

Grand Prix debut: Brazilian - Interlagos - 27/03/94
Starts: 15   **Wins:** 0
Highest finish: 4th
Pole positions: 0   **Top six finishes:** 4
Points: 7
Highest World Championship position: 13th 1994
Racing teams: Sauber 94

COMPLETE GRAND PRIX CAREER RECORD

	GP	1st	2nd	3rd	4th	5th	6th	OFP	RET	DIS	PTS	WCP
1994	15	0	0	0	1	1	2	3	8	0	7	13
Total	15	0	0	0	1	1	2	3	8	0	7	

Top six finishes: Pac (5), Fr (4), Eur (6), Jap (6)

BERTRAND GACHOT

Born: 23/12/62   **Country:** France

Grand Prix debut: French - Paul Ricard - 09/07/89
Starts: 36   **Wins:** 0
Highest finish: 5th
Pole positions: 0   **Top six finishes:** 4
Points: 5
Highest World Championship position: =12th 1991
Racing teams: Onyx 89, Rial 89, Coloni 90, Jordan 91,
Larrousse 92, Pacific 94

COMPLETE GRAND PRIX CAREER RECORD

	GP	1st	2nd	3rd	4th	5th	6th	OFP	RET	DIS	PTS	WCP
1989	5	0	0	0	0	0	0	2	3	0	0	-
1991	10	0	0	0	0	1	2	4	3	0	4	12=
1992	16	0	0	0	0	0	1	3	11	1	1	17=
1994	5	0	0	0	0	0	0	0	5	0	0	-
Total	36	0	0	0	0	1	3	9	22	1	5	

Top six finishes: 1991: Can (5), GB (6), Ger (6) 1992: Mon
(6)

JEAN-MARC GOUNON

Born: 01/01/63   **Country:** France

Grand Prix debut: Japanese - Suzuka - 24/10/93
Starts: 9   **Wins:** 0
Highest finish: 9th
Pole positions: 0
Completed races: 4
Points: 0
Highest World Championship position: None
Racing teams: Minardi 93, Simtek 94

COMPLETE GRAND PRIX CAREER RECORD

	GP	1st	2nd	3rd	4th	5th	6th	OFP	RET	DIS	PTS	WCP
1993	2	0	0	0	0	0	0	0	2	0	0	-
1994	7	0	0	0	0	0	0	4	3	0	0	-
Total	9	0	0	0	0	0	0	4	5	0	0	

Highest race positions: 1994: Fr (9), GB (16), Bel (11), Por (15)

MIKA HAKKINEN

Born: 28/09/68   **Country:** Finland

Grand Prix debut: United States - Phoenix - 10/03/91
Starts: 48   **Wins:** 0
Highest finish: 2nd
Pole positions: 0   **Top six finishes:** 14
Points: 43
Highest World Championship position: 4th 1994
Racing teams: Lotus 91-92, McLaren 93-94

COMPLETE GRAND PRIX CAREER RECORD

	GP	1st	2nd	3rd	4th	5th	6th	OFP	RET	DIS	PTS	WCP
1991	15	0	0	0	0	1	0	7	7	0	2	15=
1992	15	0	0	0	2	1	3	3	6	0	11	8
1993	3	0	0	1	0	0	0	0	2	0	4	15=
1994	15	0	1	5	0	0	0	2	7	0	26	4
Total	**48**	**0**	**1**	**6**	**2**	**2**	**3**	**12**	**22**	**0**	**43**	

Top six finishes: 1991: SM (5) 1992: Mex (6), Fr (4), GB
(6), Hun (4), Bel (6), Por (5) 1993: Jap (3) 1994: SM (3), GB
(3), Bel (2), It (3), Por (3), Eur (3)

JOHNNY HERBERT

Born: 25/06/64   **Country:** Great Britain

Grand Prix debut: Brazilian - Rio de Janeiro - 26/03/89
Starts: 63   **Wins:** 0
Highest finish: 4th
Pole positions: 0   **Top six finishes:** 8
Points: 18
Highest World Championship position: 9th 1993
Racing teams: Benetton 89, Tyrrell 89, Lotus 90-94, Ligier 94, Benetton 94

COMPLETE GRAND PRIX CAREER RECORD

	GP	1st	2nd	3rd	4th	5th	6th	OFP	RET	DIS	PTS	WCP
1989	6	0	0	0	1	1	0	3	1	0	5	14=
1990	2	0	0	0	0	0	0	0	2	0	0	-
1991	7	0	0	0	0	0	0	5	2	0	0	-
1992	16	0	0	0	0	0	2	3	11	0	2	14=
1993	16	0	0	0	3	1	0	4	8	0	11	9
1994	16	0	0	0	0	0	0	9	7	0	0	-
Total	63	0	0	0	4	2	2	24	31	0	18	

Top six finishes: 1989: Bra (4), US (5) 1992: SA (6), Fr (6) 1993: Bra (4), Eur (4), GB (4), Bel (5)

DAMON HILL

Born: 17/09/60   **Country:** Great Britain

Grand Prix debut: British - Silverstone - 12/07/92
Starts: 34   **Wins:** 9
First win: Hungarian - Hungaroring - 15/08/93
Pole positions: 4   **Top six finishes:** 23
Points: 160
Highest World Championship position: 2nd 1994
Racing teams: Brabham 92, Williams 93-94

COMPLETE GRAND PRIX CAREER RECORD

	GP	1st	2nd	3rd	4th	5th	6th	OFP	RET	DIS	PTS	WCP
1992	2	0	0	0	0	0	0	2	0	0	0	-
1993	16	3	4	3	1	0	0	1	4	0	69	3
1994	16	6	5	0	0	0	1	1	3	0	91	2
Total	34	9	9	3	1	0	1	4	7	0	160	

Grand Prix victories: 1993: Hun, Bel, It 1994: Sp, GB, Bel, It, Por, Jap

EDDIE IRVINE

Born: 10/11/65   **Country:** Great Britain

Grand Prix debut: Japanese - Suzuka - 24/10/93
Starts: 15   **Wins:** 0
Highest finish: 4th
Pole positions: 0   **Top six finishes:** 4
Points: 7
Highest World Championship position: =14th 1994
Racing teams: Jordan 93-94

COMPLETE GRAND PRIX CAREER RECORD

	GP	1st	2nd	3rd	4th	5th	6th	OFP	RET	DIS	PTS	WCP
1993	2	0	0	0	0	0	1	0	1	0	1	20=
1994	13	0	0	0	1	1	1	2	8	0	6	14=
Total	15	0	0	0	1	1	2	2	9	0	7	

Top six finishes: 1993: Jap (6) 1994: Sp (6), Eur (4), Jap (5)

UKYO KATAYAMA

Born: 29/05/63   **Country:** Japan

Grand Prix debut: South African - Kyalami - 01/03/92
Starts: 46   **Wins:** 0
Highest finish: 5th
Pole positions: 0   **Top six finishes:** 3
Points: 5
Highest World Championship position: =17th 1994
Racing teams: Larrousse 92, Tyrrell 93-94

COMPLETE GRAND PRIX CAREER RECORD

	GP	1st	2nd	3rd	4th	5th	6th	OFP	RET	DIS	PTS	WCP
1992	14	0	0	0	0	0	0	6	8	0	0	-
1993	16	0	0	0	0	0	0	5	11	0	0	-
1994	16	0	0	0	0	2	1	1	12	0	5	17=
Total	46	0	0	0	0	2	1	12	31	0	5	

Top six finishes: 1994: Bra (5), SM (5), GB (6)

PEDRO LAMY

Born: 20/03/72   **Country:** Portugal

Grand Prix debut: Italian - Monza - 12/09/93
Starts: 8   **Wins:** 0
Highest finish: 8th
Pole positions: 0
Completed races: 4
Points: 0
Highest World Championship position: None
Racing teams: Lotus 93-94

COMPLETE GRAND PRIX CAREER RECORD

	GP	1st	2nd	3rd	4th	5th	6th	OFP	RET	DIS	PTS	WCP
1993	4	0	0	0	0	0	0	1	3	0	0	-
1994	4	0	0	0	0	0	0	3	1	0	0	-
Total	8	0	0	0	0	0	0	4	4	0	0	

Highest race positions: 1993: Jap (13) 1994: Bra (10), Pac (8), Mon (11)

NICOLA LARINI

Born: 19/03/54   **Country:** Italy

Grand Prix debut: Spanish - Jerez - 27/09/87
Starts: 44   **Wins:** 0
Highest finish: 2nd
Pole positions: 0   **Top six finishes:** 1
Points: 6
Highest World Championship position: =14th 1994
Racing teams: Coloni 87, Osella 88-89, Ligier 90, Modena 91, Ferrari 92, 94

COMPLETE GRAND PRIX CAREER RECORD

	GP	1st	2nd	3rd	4th	5th	6th	OFP	RET	DIS	PTS	WCP
1987	1	0	0	0	0	0	0	0	1	0	0	-
1988	10	0	0	0	0	0	0	3	7	0	0	-
1989	8	0	0	0	0	0	0	1	6	1	0	-
1990	16	0	0	0	0	0	0	13	3	0	0	-
1991	5	0	0	0	0	0	0	3	2	0	0	-
1992	2	0	0	0	0	0	0	2	0	0	0	-
1994	2	0	1	0	0	0	0	0	1	0	6	14=
Total	**44**	**0**	**1**	**0**	**0**	**0**	**0**	**22**	**20**	**1**	**6**	

Top six finishes: 1994: SM (2)

J J LEHTO

Born: 31/01/66   **Country:** Finland

Grand Prix debut: Spanish - Jerez - 01/10/89
Starts: 62   **Wins:** 0
Highest finish: 3rd
Pole positions: 0   **Top six finishes:** 4
Points: 10
Highest World Championship position: =12th 1991
Racing teams: Onyx 89-90, Monteverdi 90, Dallara 91-92,
Sauber 93, Benetton 94, Sauber 94

COMPLETE GRAND PRIX CAREER RECORD

	GP	1st	2nd	3rd	4th	5th	6th	OFP	RET	DIS	PTS	WCP
1989	2	0	0	0	0	0	0	0	2	0	0	-
1990	5	0	0	0	0	0	0	2	3	0	0	-
1991	16	0	0	1	0	0	0	4	11	0	4	12=
1992	15	0	0	0	0	0	0	11	4	0	0	-
1993	16	0	0	0	1	1	0	5	9	0	5	13=
1994	8	0	0	0	0	0	1	3	4	0	1	24=
Total	62	0	0	1	1	1	1	25	33	0	10	

Top six finishes: 1991: SM (3) 1993: SA (5), SM (4) 1994:
Can (6)

NIGEL MANSELL

Born: 08/08/53   **Country:** Great Britain

Grand Prix debut: Austrian - Osterreichring - 17/08/80
Starts: 185   **Wins:** 31
First win: European - Brands Hatch - 06/10/85
Pole positions: 32   **Top six finishes:** 82
Points: 482
Highest World Championship position: Winner 1992
Racing teams: Lotus 80-84, Williams 85-88, Ferrari 89-90, Williams 91-92, 94

COMPLETE GRAND PRIX CAREER RECORD

	GP	1st	2nd	3rd	4th	5th	6th	OFP	RET	DIS	PTS	WCP
1980	2	0	0	0	0	0	0	0	2	0	0	-
1981	13	0	0	1	1	0	1	2	8	0	8	14
1982	13	0	0	1	1	0	0	4	7	0	7	14
1983	15	0	0	1	1	1	1	4	7	0	10	12=
1984	16	0	0	2	1	0	2	0	11	0	13	10
1985	15	2	1	0	0	2	3	2	5	0	31	6
1986	16	5	2	2	1	2	0	0	4	0	72	2
1987	14	6	0	1	0	1	1	1	4	0	61	2
1988	14	0	2	0	0	0	0	0	12	0	12	9=
1989	15	2	2	2	0	0	0	0	7	2	38	4
1990	16	1	3	1	2	0	0	2	7	0	37	5
1991	16	5	4	0	0	0	1	0	5	1	72	2
1992	16	9	3	0	0	0	0	0	4	0	108	1
1994	4	1	0	0	1	0	0	0	2	0	13	9
Total	**185**	**31**	**17**	**11**	**8**	**6**	**9**	**15**	**85**	**3**	**482**	

Grand Prix victories: 1985: Eur, SA 1986: Bel, Can, Fr, GB, Por 1987: SM, Fr, GB, Aus, Sp, Mex 1989: Bra, Hun 1990: Por 1991: Fr, GB, Ger, It, Sp 1992: SA, Mex, Bra, Sp, SM, Fr, GB, Ger, Por 1994: Aust

PIERLUIGI MARTINI

Born: 23/04/61   **Country:** Italy

Grand Prix debut: Brazilian - Rio de Janeiro - 07/04/85
Starts: 110   **Wins:** 0
Highest finish: 4th
Pole positions: 0   **Top six finishes:** 10
Points: 18
Highest World Championship position: 11th 1991
Racing teams: Toleman 84, Minardi 85, 88-91, Scuderia 92, Minardi 93-94

COMPLETE GRAND PRIX CAREER RECORD

	GP	1st	2nd	3rd	4th	5th	6th	OFP	RET	DIS	PTS	WCP
1985	15	0	0	0	0	0	0	3	12	0	0	-
1988	9	0	0	0	0	0	1	4	4	0	1	16=
1989	15	0	0	0	0	2	1	3	9	0	5	14=
1990	15	0	0	0	0	0	0	7	8	0	0	-
1991	16	0	0	0	2	0	0	7	7	0	6	11
1992	16	0	0	0	0	0	2	6	8	0	2	14=
1993	8	0	0	0	0	0	0	4	4	0	0	-
1994	16	0	0	0	0	2	0	8	6	0	4	18=
Total	**110**	**0**	**0**	**0**	**2**	**4**	**4**	**42**	**58**	**0**	**18**	

Top six finishes: 1988: US (6) 1989: GB (5), Por (5), Aust (6) 1991: SM (4), Por (4) 1992: Sp (6), SM (6) 1994: Sp (5), Fr (5)

GIANNI MORBIDELLI

Born: 13/01/68   **Country:** Italy

Grand Prix debut: Brazilian - Interlagos - 25/03/90
Starts: 50   **Wins:** 0
Highest finish: 5th
Pole positions: 0   **Top six finishes:** 3
Points: 3.5
Highest World Championship position: 22nd 1994
Racing teams: Dallara 90, Minardi 90-91, Ferrari 91,
Minardi 92, Arrows 94

COMPLETE GRAND PRIX CAREER RECORD

	GP	1st	2nd	3rd	4th	5th	6th	OFP	RET	DIS	PTS	WCP
1990	3	0	0	0	0	0	0	1	2	0	0	-
1991	16	0	0	0	0	0	1	7	8	0	0.5	24
1992	15	0	0	0	0	0	0	9	6	0	0	-
1994	16	0	0	0	0	1	1	2	12	0	3	22
Total	50	0	0	0	0	1	2	19	28	0	3.5	

Top six finishes: 1991: Aust (6) 1994: Ger (5), Bel (6)

OLIVIER PANIS

Born: 02/09/66   **Country:** France

Grand Prix debut: Brazilian - Interlagos - 27/03/94
Starts: 16   **Wins:** 0
Highest finish: 2nd
Pole positions: 0   **Top six finishes:** 3
Points: 9
Highest World Championship position: 11th 1994
Racing teams: Ligier 94

COMPLETE GRAND PRIX CAREER RECORD

	GP	1st	2nd	3rd	4th	5th	6th	OFP	RET	DIS	PTS	WCP
1994	16	0	1	0	0	1	1	11	2	0	9	11
Total	16	0	1	0	0	1	1	11	2	0	9	11

Top six finishes: 1994: Ger (2), Hun (6), Aust (5)

RICCARDO PATRESE

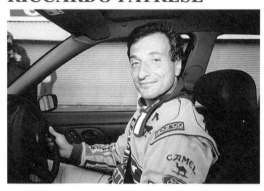

Born: 17/04/54 **Country:** Italy

Grand Prix debut: Monaco - Monte Carlo - 22/05/77
Starts: 256 **Wins:** 6
First win: Monaco - Monte Carlo - 23/05/1982
Pole positions: 8 **Top six finishes:** 73
Points: 281
Highest World Championship position: 2nd 1992
Racing teams: Shadow 77, Arrows 78-81, Brabham 82-83, Alfa Romeo 84-85, Brabham 86-87, Williams 87-92, Benetton 93

COMPLETE GRAND PRIX CAREER RECORD

	GP	1st	2nd	3rd	4th	5th	6th	OFP	RET	DIS	PTS	WCP
1977	9	0	0	0	0	0	1	4	4	0	1	19=
1978	14	0	1	0	1	0	2	3	7	0	11	11=
1979	14	0	0	0	0	1	0	5	8	0	2	19=
1980	14	0	1	0	0	0	1	5	7	0	7	9
1981	15	0	1	1	0	0	0	4	9	0	10	11=
1982	15	1	1	1	0	1	0	1	10	0	21	10
1983	15	1	0	1	0	0	0	3	10	0	13	9
1984	16	0	0	1	1	0	1	3	10	0	8	13
1985	16	0	0	0	0	0	0	4	12	0	0	-
1986	16	0	0	0	0	0	2	3	11	0	2	15=
1987	16	0	0	1	0	1	0	5	9	0	6	13
1988	16	0	0	0	1	1	3	3	8	0	8	11
1989	16	0	4	2	2	1	0	1	6	0	40	3
1990	16	1	0	0	2	3	2	4	4	0	23	7
1991	16	2	2	4	0	3	0	0	5	0	53	3
1992	16	1	6	2	0	1	0	1	5	0	56	2
1993	16	0	1	1	1	3	1	3	6	0	20	5
Total	**256**	**6**	**17**	**14**	**8**	**15**	**13**	**52**	**131**	**0**	**281**	

Grand Prix victories: 1982: Mon 1983: SA 1990: SM 1991: Mex, Por 1992: Jap

ALAIN PROST

Born: 24/02/55 **Country:** France

Grand Prix debut: Argentine - Buenos Aires - 13/01/80
Starts: 199 **Wins:** 51
First win: French - Dijon - 05/07/81
Pole positions: 32 **Top six finishes:** 128
Points: 798.5
Highest World Championship position: Winner 1985, 1986, 1989, 1993
Racing teams: McLaren 80, Renault 81-83, McLaren 84-89, Ferrari 90-91, Williams 93

COMPLETE GRAND PRIX CAREER RECORD

	GP	1st	2nd	3rd	4th	5th	6th	OFP	RET	DIS	PTS	WCP
1980	11	0	0	0	0	1	3	3	4	0	5	15=
1981	15	3	2	1	0	0	0	0	9	0	43	5
1982	16	2	2	0	1	0	1	3	7	0	34	4
1983	15	4	2	1	1	1	0	3	3	0	57	2
1984	16	7	1	1	1	0	0	1	5	0	71.5	2
1985	16	5	2	4	1	0	0	0	3	1	76	1
1986	16	4	4	3	0	0	2	0	2	1	74	1
1987	16	3	1	3	0	0	1	4	4	0	46	4
1988	16	7	7	0	0	0	0	0	2	0	105	2
1989	16	4	6	1	1	1	0	0	3	0	81	1
1990	16	5	2	2	2	1	0	0	4	0	73	2
1991	14	0	3	2	2	1	0	0	6	0	34	5
1993	16	7	3	2	1	0	0	2	1	0	99	1
Total	**199**	**51**	**35**	**20**	**10**	**5**	**7**	**16**	**53**	**2**	**798.5**	

Grand Prix victories: 1981: Fr, Dut, It 1982: SA, Bra 1983: Fr, Bel, GB, Aus 1984: Bra, SM, Mon, Ger, Dut, Eur, Por 1985: Bra, Mon, GB, Aus, It 1986: SM, Mon, Aus, Aust 1987: Bra, Bel, Por 1988: Bra, Mon, Mex, Fr, Por, Sp, Aust 1989: US, Fr, GB, It 1990: Bra, Mex, Fr, GB, Sp 1993: SA, SM, Sp, Can, Fr, GB, Ger

MICHAEL SCHUMACHER

Born: 03/01/69   **Country:** Germany

Grand Prix debut: Belgian - Spa - 25/08/91
Starts: 52   **Wins:** 10
First win: Belgian - Spa - 30/08/92
Pole positions: 6   **Top six finishes:** 33
Points: 201
Highest World Championship position: Winner 1994
Racing teams: Jordan 91, Benetton 91-94

COMPLETE GRAND PRIX CAREER RECORD

	GP	1st	2nd	3rd	4th	5th	6th	OFP	RET	DIS	PTS	WCP
1991	6	0	0	0	0	1	2	0	3	0	4	12=
1992	16	1	3	4	3	0	0	1	4	0	53	3
1993	16	1	5	3	0	0	0	0	7	0	52	4
1994	14	8	2	0	0	0	0	0	2	2	92	1
Total	52	10	10	7	3	1	2	1	16	2	201	

Grand Prix victories: 1992: Bel 1993: Por 1994: Bra, Pac, SM, Mon, Can, Fr, Hun, Eur

AYRTON SENNA

Born: 21/03/60   **Died:** 01/05/94   **Country:** Brazil

Grand Prix debut: Brazilian - Rio de Janeiro - 25/03/84
Starts: 161   **Wins:** 41
First win: Portuguese - Estoril - 21/04/85
Pole positions: 65   **Top six finishes:** 96
Points: 614
Highest World Championship position: Winner 1988, 1990, 1991
Racing teams: Toleman 84, Lotus 85-87, McLaren 88-93, Williams 94

COMPLETE GRAND PRIX CAREER RECORD

	GP	1st	2nd	3rd	4th	5th	6th	OFP	RET	DIS	PTS	WCP
1984	14	0	1	2	0	0	2	1	8	0	13	9
1985	16	2	2	2	0	0	0	3	7	0	38	4
1986	16	2	4	2	1	1	0	0	6	0	55	4
1987	16	2	4	2	1	2	0	1	3	1	57	3
1988	16	8	3	0	1	0	1	1	1	1	94	1
1989	16	6	1	0	0	0	0	2	6	1	60	2
1990	16	6	2	3	0	0	0	1	4	0	78	1
1991	16	7	3	2	1	1	0	1	1	0	96	1
1992	16	3	1	3	0	1	0	1	7	0	50	4
1993	16	5	2	0	3	1	0	1	4	0	73	2
1994	3	0	0	0	0	0	0	0	3	0	0	-
Total	161	41	23	16	7	6	3	12	50	3	614	

Grand Prix victories: 1985: Por, Bel 1986: Sp, Det 1987: Mon, US 1988: SM, Can, US, GB, Ger, Hun, Bel, Jap 1989: SM, Mon, Mex, Ger, Bel, Sp 1990: US, Mon, Can, Ger, Bel, It 1991: US, Bra, SM, Mon, Hun, Bel, Aust 1992: Mon, Hun, It 1993: Bra, Eur, Mon, Jap, Aust

AGURI SUZUKI

Born: 08/09/60   **Country:** Japan

Grand Prix debut: Japanese - Suzuka - 30/10/88
Starts: 59   **Wins:** 0
Highest finish: 3rd
Pole positions: 0   **Top six finishes:** 4
Points: 7
Highest World Championship position: =10th 1990
Racing teams: Lola 88, Zakspeed 89, Larrousse 90-91,
Footwork 92-93, Jordan 94

COMPLETE GRAND PRIX CAREER RECORD

	GP	1st	2nd	3rd	4th	5th	6th	OFP	RET	DIS	PTS	WCP
1988	1	0	0	0	0	0	0	1	0	0	0	-
1990	16	0	0	1	0	0	2	3	10	0	6	10=
1991	11	0	0	0	0	0	1	0	10	0	1	18=
1992	14	0	0	0	0	0	0	9	5	0	0	-
1993	16	0	0	0	0	0	0	5	11	0	0	-
1994	1	0	0	0	0	0	0	0	1	0	0	-
Total	59	0	0	1	0	0	3	18	37	0	7	

Top six finishes: 1990: GB (6), Sp (6), Jap (3) 1991: US (6)

JOS VERSTAPPEN

Born: 04/03/72   **Country:** Holland

Grand Prix debut: Brazilian - Interlagos - 27/03/94
Starts: 10   **Wins:** 0
Highest finish: 3rd
Pole positions: 0   **Top six finishes:** 3
Points: 10
Highest World Championship position: 10th 1994
Racing teams: Benetton

COMPLETE GRAND PRIX CAREER RECORD

	GP	1st	2nd	3rd	4th	5th	6th	OFP	RET	DIS	PTS	WCP
1994	10	0	0	2	0	1	0	1	6	0	10	10
Total	10	0	0	2	0	1	0	1	6	0	10	10

Top six finishes: 1994: Hun (3), Bel (3), Por (5)

DEREK WARWICK

Born: 27/08/54   **Country:** Great Britain

Grand Prix debut: Las Vegas - Caesar's Palace - 17/10/81
Starts: 147   **Wins:** 0
Highest finish: 2nd
Pole positions: 0   **Top six finishes:** 30
Points: 71
Highest World Championship position: 7th 1984, =7th 1988
Racing teams: Toleman 81-83, Renault 84-85, Brabham 86, Arrows 87-89, Lotus 90, Footwork 93

COMPLETE GRAND PRIX CAREER RECORD

	GP	1st	2nd	3rd	4th	5th	6th	OFP	RET	DIS	PTS	WCP
1981	1	0	0	0	0	0	0	0	1	0	0	-
1982	11	0	0	0	0	0	0	2	9	0	0	-
1983	15	0	0	0	2	1	1	2	9	0	9	14
1984	16	0	2	2	1	0	0	1	10	0	23	7
1985	15	0	0	0	0	2	1	4	8	0	5	13=
1986	10	0	0	0	0	0	0	4	6	0	0	-
1987	16	0	0	0	0	1	1	4	10	0	3	16=
1988	16	0	0	0	4	2	1	3	6	0	17	7=
1989	15	0	0	0	0	2	3	3	7	0	7	10
1990	16	0	0	0	0	1	1	5	9	0	3	14=
1993	16	0	0	0	1	0	1	9	5	0	4	15=
Total	147	0	2	2	8	9	9	37	80	0	71	

Top six finishes: 1983: Dut (4), It (6), Eur (5), SA (4) 1984: SA (3), Bel (2), SM (4), GB (2), Ger (3) 1985: Mon (5), GB (5), Bel (6) 1987: GB (5), Hun (6) 1988: Bra (4), Mon (4), Mex (5), GB (6), Bel (5), It (4), Por (4) 1989: Bra (5), SM (5), Ger (6), Bel (6), Jap (6) 1990: Can (6), Hun (5) 1993: GB (6), Hun (4)

KARL WENDLINGER

Born: 20/12/68   **Country:** Austria

Grand Prix debut: Japanese - Suzuka - 20/10/91
Starts: 35   **Wins:** 0
Highest finish: 4th
Pole positions: 0   **Top six finishes:** 7
Points: 14
Highest World Championship position: =11th 1993
Racing teams: Leyton House 91, March 92, Sauber 93-94

COMPLETE GRAND PRIX CAREER RECORD

	GP	1st	2nd	3rd	4th	5th	6th	OFP	RET	DIS	PTS	WCP
1991	2	0	0	0	0	0	0	1	1	0	0	-
1992	14	0	0	0	1	0	0	5	8	0	3	12=
1993	16	0	0	0	1	1	2	3	9	0	7	11=
1994	3	0	0	0	1	0	1	0	1	0	4	18=
Total	35	0	0	0	3	1	3	9	19	0	14	

Top six finishes: 1992: Can (4) 1993: Can (6), Hun (6), It (4), Por (5) 1994: Bra (6), SM (4)

ALESSANDRO ZANARDI

Born: 23/10/66   **Country:** Italy

Grand Prix debut: Spanish - Barcelona - 29/09/91
Starts: 25   **Wins:** 0
Highest finish: 6th
Pole positions: 0   **Top six finishes:** 1
Points: 1
Highest World Championship position: =20th 1993
Racing teams: Jordan 91, Minardi 92, Lotus 93-94

COMPLETE GRAND PRIX CAREER RECORD

	GP	1st	2nd	3rd	4th	5th	6th	OFP	RET	DIS	PTS	WCP
1991	3	0	0	0	0	0	0	2	1	0	0	-
1992	1	0	0	0	0	0	0	0	1	0	0	-
1993	11	0	0	0	0	0	1	3	7	0	1	20=
1994	10	0	0	0	0	0	0	4	6	0	0	-
Total	25	0	0	0	0	0	1	9	15	0	1	

Top six finishes: 1993: Bra (6)

OTHER 1994 DRIVERS

Name: Philippe Adams
Born: 19/11/69
Country: Belgium
Grand Prix debut: Belgian - Spa Francorchamps - 28/08/94
Starts: 2
Racing team: Lotus
1994 races: Bel (ret), Por (16)

Name: Jean-Denis Deletraz
Born: 01/10/63
Country: Switzerland
Grand Prix debut: Australian - Adelaide - 13/11/94
Starts: 1
Racing team: Larrousse
1994 races: Aust (ret)

Name: 'Taki' Inoue
Born: 05/09/63
Country: Japan
Grand Prix debut: Japanese - Suzuka - 06/11/94
Starts: 1
Racing team: Simtek
1994 races: Jap (ret)

Name: Franck Lagorce
Born: 01/09/68
Country: France
Grand Prix debut: Japanese - Suzuka - 06/11/94
Starts: 2
Racing team: Ligier
1994 races: Jap (Ret), Aust (11)

Name: Hideki Noda
Born: 07/03/69
Country: Japan
Grand Prix debut: European - Jerez - 16/10/94
Starts: 3
Racing team: Larrousse
1994 races: Eur (ret), Jap (ret), Aust (ret)

Name: Roland Ratzenberger
Born: 04/07/62 Died: 30/04/1994
Country: Austria
Grand Prix debut: Pacific - Aida - 17/04/94
Starts: 1
Racing team: Simtek
1994 races: Pac (11)

Name: Mika Salo
Born: 30/11/66
Country: Finland
Grand Prix debut: Japanese - Suzuka - 06/11/94
Starts: 2
Racing team: Lotus
1994 races: Jap (10), Aust (ret)

Name: Domenico 'Mimmo' Schiattarella
Born: 17/11/67
Country: Italy
Grand Prix debut: European - Jerez - 16/10/94
Starts: 2
Racing team: Simtek
1994 races: Eur (19), Aust (ret)

DRIVERS' CHAMPIONSHIP POINTS SCORING SYSTEMS

Pos	1950-1959 Pts	1960 Pts	1961-1990 Pts	1991-1994 Pts
1st	8	8	9	10
2nd	6	6	6	6
3rd	4	4	4	4
4th	3	3	3	3
5th	2	2	2	2
6th		1	1	1

From 1950-1959 1 point was also awarded for the fastest lap.

Races counted per year

1950-1953	Top 4 races
1954-1957	Top 5 races
1958	Top 6 races
1959	Top 5 races
1960	Top 6 races
1961	Top 5 races
1962	Top 5 races
1963-1965	Top 6 races
1966	Top 5 races
1967-1978	Two part Championship - Worst result discarded from each half
1979	Two part Championship - best four results in each half
1980	Two part Championship - best five results in each half
1981-1990	Top 11 races
1991-1994	All races

CONSTRUCTORS' CHAMPIONSHIP POINTS SCORING SYSTEM

From its introduction in 1958 until 1978 the Constructors' Championship points were awarded as above. However, only the highest placed car of each manufacturer counted towards the Championship. This system was changed in 1979, to the current one, whereby all cars finishing in the top six score points.

1995 TEAMS AND DRIVERS

Teams	**Drivers**
Arrows-Hart	Gianni Morbidelli
	Taki Inoue
Benetton-Renault	Michael Schumacher
	Johnny Herbert
Ferrari	Gerhard Berger
	Jean Alesi
Forti-Ford	Pedro Diniz
	Andrea Montermini*
Jordan-Peugeot	Rubens Barrichello
	Eddie Irvine
Larrousse	Erik Comas
	TBA
Ligier-Mugen Honda	Olivier Panis
	Martin Brundle
	Aguri Suzuki
McLaren-Mercedes	Nigel Mansell
	Mika Hakkinen
Minardi-Ford	Pierluigi Martini
	Luca Badoer
Pacific Ford	Bertrand Gachot
	Pedro Lamy*
Sauber-Ford	Karl Wendlinger
	Heinz-Harald Frentzen
Simtek-Ford	Hedeki Noda
	Jos Verstappen
	Domenico Schiattarella
Tyrrell-Yamaha	Ukyo Katayama
	Mika Salo
Williams-Renault	Damon Hill
	David Coulthard

* Pending confirmation

PRE-SEASON HIGHLIGHTS

❑ **Jordan** sign engine deal with **Peugeot**

❑ **McLaren** sign engine deal with **Mercedes**

❑ **Williams** choose **David Coulthard** ahead of **Nigel Mansell**

❑ **Lotus** announce they will not be entering the 1995 World Championship due to financial difficulties. It is the first Formula 1 season they will miss since their formation in 1958

❑ **Martin Brundle** signs for **Ligier**

❑ The launch of **Forti-Ford,** the only new manufacturer for the 1995 season. The Brazilian **Pedro Diniz** will drive for them.

❑ **Nigel Mansell** signs for **McLaren**

❑ **Lotus** announce merger deal with **Pacific**. Their new team will be known as **Pacific Team Lotus**

❑ **Jos Verstappen** will drive for **Simtek** in 1995, although he remains under contract with Benetton

❑ **Larrousse** may miss the first two races of 1995 due to a lack of sponsorship.

1995 FORMULA ONE CALENDAR

1	26/03/95	Brazil	Interlagos
2	09/04/95	Argentina	Buenos Aires
3	30/04/95	San Marino	Imola
4	14/05/95	Spain	Barcelona
5	28/05/95	Monaco	Monte Carlo
6	11/06/95	Canada	Montreal
7	02/07/95	France	Magny-Cours
8	16/07/95	Britain	Silverstone
9	30/07/95	Germany	Hockenheim
10	27/08/95	Belgium	Spa
11	10/09/95	Italy	Monza
12	24/09/95	Portugal	Estoril
13	01/10/95	Europe	Nurburgring
14	22/10/95	Pacific	Aida
15	29/10/95	Japan	Suzuka
16	12/11/95	Australia	Adelaide

In the case of any of the above being cancelled there will be a Hungarian Grand Prix on 13 August.

GRAND PRIX WINNERS 1950-1994

1950

British	Silverstone	13/05/50	G. Farina	Alfa Romeo
Monaco	Monte Carlo	21/05/50	J.M. Fangio	Alfa Romeo
Swiss	Bremgarten	04/06/50	G. Farina	Alfa Romeo
Belgian	Spa	18/06/50	J.M. Fangio	Alfa Romeo
French	Reims	02/07/50	J.M. Fangio	Alfa Romeo
Italian	Monza	03/09/50	G. Farina	Alfa Romeo

1951

Swiss	Bremgarten	27/05/51	J.M. Fangio	Alfa Romeo
Belgian	Spa	17/06/51	G. Farina	Alfa Romeo
French	Reims	01/07/51	L. Fagioli	Alfa Romeo
			J.M.Fangio	
British	Silverstone	14/07/51	J.F. Gonzalez	Ferrari
German	Nurburgring	29/07/51	A. Ascari	Ferrari
Italian	Monza	16/09/51	A. Ascari	Ferrari
Spanish	Pedralbes	28/10/51	J.M. Fangio	Alfa Romeo

1952

Swiss	Bremgarten	18/05/52	P. Taruffi	Ferrari
Belgian	Spa	22/06/52	A. Ascari	Ferrari
French	Rouen	06/07/52	A. Ascari	Ferrari
British	Silverstone	19/07/52	A. Ascari	Ferrari
German	Nurburgring	03/08/52	A. Ascari	Ferrari
Dutch	Zandvoort	17/08/52	A. Ascari	Ferrari
Italian	Monza	07/09/52	A. Ascari	Ferrari

1953

Argentine	Buenos Aires	18/01/53	A. Ascari	Ferrari
Dutch	Zandvoort	07/06/53	A. Ascari	Ferrari
Belgian	Spa	21/06/53	A. Ascari	Ferrari
French	Reims	05/07/53	M. Hawthorn	Ferrari
British	Silverstone	18/07/53	A. Ascari	Ferrari
German	Nurburgring	02/08/53	G. Farina	Ferrari
Swiss	Bremgarten	23/08/53	A. Ascari	Ferrari
Italian	Monza	13/09/53	J.M. Fangio	Maserati

1954

Argentine	Buenos Aires	17/01/54	J.M. Fangio	Maserati
Belgian	Spa	20/06/54	J.M. Fangio	Maserati
French	Reims	04/07/54	J.M. Fangio	Mercedes
British	Silverstone	17/07/54	J.F. Gonzalez	Ferrari
German	Nurburgring	01/08/54	J.M. Fangio	Mercedes
Swiss	Bremgarten	22/08/54	J.M. Fangio	Mercedes
Italian	Monza	05/09/54	J.M. Fangio	Mercedes
Spanish	Pedralbes	24/10/54	M. Hawthorn	Ferrari

1955

Argentine	Buenos Aires	16/01/55	J.M. Fangio	Mercedes
Monaco	Monte Carlo	22/05/55	M. Trintignant	Ferrari
Belgian	Spa	05/06/55	J.M. Fangio	Mercedes
Dutch	Zandvoort	19/06/55	J.M. Fangio	Mercedes
British	Aintree	16/07/55	S. Moss	Mercedes

| Italian | Monza | 11/09/55 | J.M. Fangio | Mercedes |

1956

Argentine	Buenos Aires	22/01/56	L. Musso	Lancia-Ferrari
			J.M. Fangio	
Monaco	Monte Carlo	13/05/56	S. Moss	Maserati
Belgian	Spa	03/06/56	P. Collins	Lancia-Ferrari
French	Reims	01/07/56	P. Collins	Lancia-Ferrari
British	Silverstone	14/07/56	J.M. Fangio	Lancia-Ferrari
German	Nurburgring	05/08/56	J.M. Fangio	Lancia-Ferrari
Italian	Monza	02/09/56	S. Moss	Maserati

1957

Argentine	Buenos Aires	13/01/57	J.M. Fangio	Maserati
Monaco	Monte Carlo	19/05/57	J.M. Fangio	Maserati
French	Rouen	07/07/57	J.M. Fangio	Maserati
British	Aintree	20/07/57	T. Brooks	Vanwall
			S. Moss	
German	Nurburgring	04/08/57	J.M. Fangio	Maserati
Pescara	Pescara	18/08/57	S. Moss	Vanwall
Italian	Monza	08/09/57	S. Moss	Vanwall

1958

Argentine	Buenos Aires	19/01/58	S. Moss	Cooper-Climax
Monaco	Monte Carlo	18/05/58	M. Trintignant	Cooper-Climax
Dutch	Zandvoort	26/05/58	S. Moss	Vanwall
Belgian	Spa	15/06/58	T. Brooks	Vanwall
French	Reims	06/07/58	M. Hawthorn	Ferrari
British	Silverstone	19/07/58	P. Collins	Ferrari
German	Nurburgring	03/08/58	T. Brooks	Vanwall
Portuguese	Oporto	24/08/58	S. Moss	Vanwall
Italian	Monza	07/09/58	T. Brooks	Vanwall
Moroccan	Casablanca	19/10/58	S. Moss	Vanwall

1959

Monaco	Monte Carlo	10/05/59	J. Brabham	Cooper-Climax
Dutch	Zandvoort	31/05/59	J. Bonnier	BRM
French	Reims	05/07/59	T. Brooks	Ferrari
British	Aintree	18/07/59	J. Brabham	Cooper-Climax
German	Avus	02/08/59	T. Brooks	Ferrari
Portuguese	Monsanto	23/08/59	S. Moss	Cooper-Climax
Italian	Monza	13/09/59	S. Moss	Cooper-Climax
U. States	Sebring	12/12/59	B. McLaren	Cooper-Climax

1960

Argentine	Buenos Aires	07/02/60	B. McLaren	Cooper-Climax
Monaco	Monte Carlo	29/05/60	S. Moss	Lotus-Climax
Dutch	Zandvoort	06/06/60	J. Brabham	Cooper-Climax
Belgian	Spa	19/06/60	J. Brabham	Cooper-Climax
French	Reims	03/07/60	J. Brabham	Cooper-Climax
British	Silverstone	16/07/60	J. Brabham	Cooper-Climax
Portuguese	Oporto	14/08/60	J. Brabham	Cooper-Climax
Italian	Monza	04/09/60	P. Hill	Ferrari
U. States	Riverside	20/11/60	S. Moss	Lotus-Climax

1961

| Monaco | Monte Carlo | 14/05/61 | S. Moss | Lotus-Climax |

Dutch	Zandvoort	22/05/61	W. von Trips	Ferrari
Belgian	Spa	18/06/61	P. Hill	Ferrari
French	Reims	02/07/61	G. Baghetti	Ferrari
British	Aintree	15/07/61	W. von Trips	Ferrari
German	Nurburgring	06/08/61	S. Moss	Lotus-Climax
Italian	Monza	10/09/61	P. Hill	Ferrari
U. States	Watkins Glen	08/10/61	I. Ireland	Lotus-Climax

1962

Dutch	Zandvoort	20/05/62	G. Hill	BRM
Monaco	Monte Carlo	03/06/62	B. McLaren	Cooper-Climax
Belgian	Spa	17/06/62	J. Clark	Lotus-Climax
French	Rouen	08/07/62	D. Gurney	Porsche
British	Aintree	21/07/62	J. Clark	Lotus-Climax
German	Nurburgring	05/08/62	G. Hill	BRM
Italian	Monza	16/09/62	G. Hill	BRM
U. States	Watkins Glen	07/10/62	J. Clark	Lotus-Climax
S. African	East London	29/12/62	G. Hill	BRM

1963

Monaco	Monte Carlo	26/05/63	G. Hill	BRM
Belgian	Spa	09/06/63	J. Clark	Lotus-Climax
Dutch	Zandvoort	23/06/63	J. Clark	Lotus-Climax
French	Reims	30/06/63	J. Clark	Lotus-Climax
British	Silverstone	20/07/63	J. Clark	Lotus-Climax
German	Nurburgring	04/08/63	J. Surtees	Ferrari
Italian	Monza	08/09/63	J. Clark	Lotus-Climax
U. States	Watkins Glen	06/10/63	G. Hill	BRM
Mexican	Mexico City	27/10/63	J. Clark	Lotus-Climax
S. African	East London	28/12/63	J. Clark	Lotus-Climax

1964

Monaco	Monte Carlo	10/05/64	G. Hill	BRM
Dutch	Zandvoort	24/05/64	J. Clark	Lotus-Climax
Belgian	Spa	14/06/64	J. Clark	Lotus-Climax
French	Rouen	28/06/64	D. Gurney	Brabham-Climax
British	Brands Hatch	11/07/64	J. Clark	Lotus-Climax
German	Nurburgring	02/08/64	J. Surtees	Ferrari
Austrian	Zeltweg	23/08/64	L. Bandini	Ferrari
Italian	Monza	06/09/64	J. Surtees	Ferrari
U. States	Watkins Glen	04/10/64	G. Hill	BRM
Mexican	Mexico City	25/10/64	D. Gurney	Brabham-Climax

1965

S. African	East London	01/01/65	J. Clark	Lotus-Climax
Monaco	Monte Carlo	30/05/65	G. Hill	BRM
Belgian	Spa	13/06/65	J. Clark	Lotus-Climax
French	Clermont-Ferrand	27/06/65	J. Clark	Lotus-Climax
British	Silverstone	10/07/65	J. Clark	Lotus-Climax
Dutch	Zandvoort	18/07/65	J. Clark	Lotus-Climax
German	Nurburgring	01/08/65	J. Clark	Lotus-Climax
Italian	Monza	12/09/65	J. Stewart	BRM
U. States	Watkins Glen	03/10/65	G. Hill	BRM
Mexican	Mexico City	24/10/65	R. Ginther	Honda

1966

Monaco	Monte Carlo	22/05/66	J. Stewart	BRM
Belgian	Spa	12/06/66	J. Surtees	Ferrari
French	Reims	03/07/66	J. Brabham	Brabham-Repco
British	Brands Hatch	16/07/66	J. Brabham	Brabham-Repco
Dutch	Zandvoort	24/07/66	J. Brabham	Brabham-Repco
German	Nurburgring	07/08/66	J. Brabham	Brabham-Repco
Italian	Monza	04/09/66	L. Scarfiotti	Ferrari
U. States	Watkins Glen	02/10/66	J. Clark	Lotus-BRM
Mexican	Mexico City	23/10/66	J. Surtees	Cooper-Maserati

1967

S. African	Kyalami	02/01/67	P. Rodriguez	Cooper-Maserati
Monaco	Monte Carlo	07/05/67	D. Hulme	Brabham-Repco
Dutch	Zandvoort	04/06/67	J. Clark	Lotus-Ford
Belgian	Spa	18/06/67	D. Gurney	Eagle-Weslake
French	Le Mans	02/07/67	J. Brabham	Brabham-Repco
British	Silverstone	15/07/67	J. Clark	Lotus-Ford
German	Nurburgring	06/08/67	D. Hulme	Brabham-Repco
Canadian	Mosport Park	27/08/67	J. Brabham	Brabham-Repco
Italian	Monza	10/09/67	J. Surtees	Honda
U. States	Watkins Glen	01/10/67	J. Clark	Lotus-Ford
Mexican	Mexico City	22/10/67	J. Clark	Lotus-Ford

1968

S. African	Kyalami	01/01/68	J. Clark	Lotus-Ford
Spanish	Jarama	12/05/68	G. Hill	Lotus-Ford
Monaco	Monte Carlo	26/05/68	G. Hill	Lotus-Ford
Belgian	Spa	09/06/68	B. McLaren	McLaren-Ford
Dutch	Zandvoort	23/06/68	J. Stewart	Matra-Ford
French	Rouen	07/07/68	J. Ickx	Ferrari
British	Brands Hatch	20/07/68	J. Siffert	Lotus-Ford
German	Nurburgring	04/08/68	J. Stewart	Matra-Ford
Italian	Monza	08/09/68	D. Hulme	McLaren-Ford
Canadian	St Jovite	22/09/68	D. Hulme	McLaren-Ford
U. States	Watkins Glen	06/10/68	J. Stewart	Matra-Ford
Mexican	Mexico City	03/11/68	G. Hill	Lotus-Ford

1969

S. African	Kyalami	01/03/69	J. Stewart	Matra-Ford
Spanish	Montjuich Park	04/05/69	J. Stewart	Matra-Ford
Monaco	Monte Carlo	18/05/69	G. Hill	Lotus-Ford
Dutch	Zandvoort	21/06/69	J. Stewart	Matra-Ford
French	Clermont-Ferrand	06/07/69	J. Stewart	Matra-Ford
British	Silverstone	19/07/69	J. Stewart	Matra-Ford
German	Nurburgring	03/08/69	J. Ickx	Brabham-Ford
Italian	Monza	07/09/69	J. Stewart	Matra-Ford
Canadian	Mosport Park	20/09/69	J. Ickx	Brabham-Ford
U. States	Watkins Glen	05/10/69	J. Rindt	Lotus-Ford
Mexican	Mexico City	19/10/69	D. Hulme	McLaren-Ford

1970

S. African	Kyalami	07/03/70	J. Brabham	Brabham-Ford
Spanish	Jarama	19/04/70	J. Stewart	March-Ford
Monaco	Monte Carlo	10/05/70	J. Rindt	Lotus-Ford

Belgian	Spa	07/06/70	P. Rodriguez	BRM
Dutch	Zandvoort	21/06/70	J. Rindt	Lotus-Ford
French	Clermont-Ferrand	05/07/70	J. Rindt	Lotus-Ford
British	Brands Hatch	18/07/70	J. Rindt	Lotus-Ford
German	Hockenheim	02/08/70	J. Rindt	Lotus-Ford
Austrian	Osterreichring	16/08/70	J. Ickx	Ferrari
Italian	Monza	06/09/70	C. Regazzoni	Ferrari
Canadian	St Jovite	20/09/70	J. Ickx	Ferrari
U. States	Watkins Glen	04/10/70	E. Fittipaldi	Lotus-Ford
Mexican	Mexico City	25/10/70	J. Ickx	Ferrari

1971

S. African	Kyalami	06/03/71	M. Andretti	Ferrari
Spanish	Montjuich Park	18/04/71	J. Stewart	Tyrrell-Ford
Monaco	Monte Carlo	23/05/71	J. Stewart	Tyrrell-Ford
Dutch	Zandvoort	20/06/71	J. Ickx	Ferrari
French	Paul Ricard	04/07/71	J. Stewart	Tyrrell-Ford
British	Silverstone	17/07/71	J. Stewart	Tyrrell-Ford
German	Nurburgring	01/08/71	J. Stewart	Tyrrell-Ford
Austrian	Osterreichring	15/08/71	J. Siffert	BRM
Italian	Monza	05/09/71	P. Gethin	BRM
Canadian	Mosport Park	19/09/71	J. Stewart	Tyrrell-Ford
U. States	Watkins Glen	03/10/71	F. Cevert	Tyrrell-Ford

1972

Argentine	Buenos Aires	23/01/72	J. Stewart	Tyrrell-Ford
S. African	Kyalami	04/03/72	D. Hulme	McLaren-Ford
Spanish	Jarama	01/05/72	E. Fittipaldi	Lotus-Ford
Monaco	Monte Carlo	14/05/72	J.P. Beltoise	BRM
Belgian	Nivelles	04/06/72	E. Fittipaldi	Lotus-Ford
French	Clermont-Ferrand	02/07/72	J. Stewart	Tyrrell-Ford
British	Brands Hatch	15/07/72	E. Fittipaldi	Lotus-Ford
German	Nurburgring	30/07/72	J. Ickx	Ferrari
Austrian	Osterreichring	13/08/72	E. Fittipaldi	Lotus-Ford
Italian	Monza	10/09/72	E. Fittipaldi	Lotus-Ford
Canadian	Mosport Park	24/09/72	J. Stewart	Tyrrell-Ford
U. States	Watkins Glen	08/10/72	J. Stewart	Tyrrell-Ford

1973

Argentine	Buenos Aires	28/01/73	E. Fittipaldi	Lotus-Ford
Brazilian	Interlagos	11/02/73	E. Fittipaldi	Lotus-Ford
S. African	Kyalami	03/03/73	J. Stewart	Tyrrell-Ford
Spanish	Montjuich Park	29/04/73	E. Fittipaldi	Lotus-Ford
Belgian	Zolder	20/05/73	J. Stewart	Tyrrell-Ford
Monaco	Monte Carlo	03/06/73	J. Stewart	Tyrrell-Ford
Swedish	Anderstorp	17/06/73	D. Hulme	McLaren-Ford
French	Paul Ricard	01/07/73	R. Peterson	Lotus-Ford
British	Silverstone	14/07/73	P. Revson	McLaren-Ford
Dutch	Zandvoort	29/07/73	J. Stewart	Tyrrell-Ford
German	Nurburgring	05/08/73	J. Stewart	Tyrrell-Ford
Austrian	Osterreichring	19/08/73	R. Peterson	Lotus-Ford
Italian	Monza	09/09/73	R. Peterson	Lotus-Ford
Canadian	Mosport Park	23/09/73	P. Revson	McLaren-Ford
U. States	Watkins Glen	07/10/73	R. Peterson	Lotus-Ford

1974

Argentine	Buenos Aires	13/01/74	D. Hulme	McLaren-Ford
Brazilian	Interlagos	27/01/74	E. Fittipaldi	McLaren-Ford
S. African	Kyalami	30/03/74	C. Reutemann	Brabham-Ford
Spanish	Jarama	28/04/74	N. Lauda	Ferrari
Belgian	Nivelles	12/05/74	E. Fittipaldi	McLaren-Ford
Monaco	Monte Carlo	26/05/74	R. Peterson	Lotus-Ford
Swedish	Anderstorp	09/06/74	J. Scheckter	Tyrrell-Ford
Dutch	Zandvoort	23/06/74	N. Lauda	Ferrari
French	Dijon	07/07/74	R. Peterson	Lotus-Ford
British	Brands Hatch	20/07/74	J. Scheckter	Tyrrell-Ford
German	Nurburgring	04/08/74	C. Regazzoni	Ferrari
Austrian	Osterreichring	18/08/74	C. Reutemann	Brabham-Ford
Italian	Monza	08/09/74	R. Peterson	Lotus-Ford
Canadian	Mosport Park	22/09/74	E. Fittipaldi	McLaren-Ford
U. States	Watkins Glen	06/10/74	C. Reutemann	Brabham-Ford

1975

Argentine	Buenos Aires	12/01/75	E. Fittipaldi	McLaren-Ford
Brazilian	Interlagos	26/01/75	C. Pace	Brabham-Ford
S. African	Kyalami	01/03/75	J. Scheckter	Tyrrell-Ford
Spanish	Montjuich Park	27/04/75	J. Mass	McLaren-Ford
Monaco	Monte Carlo	11/05/75	N. Lauda	Ferrari
Belgian	Zolder	25/05/75	N. Lauda	Ferrari
Swedish	Anderstorp	08/06/75	N. Lauda	Ferrari
Dutch	Zandvoort	22/06/75	J. Hunt	Hesketh-Ford
French	Paul Ricard	06/07/75	N. Lauda	Ferrari
British	Silverstone	19/07/75	E. Fittipaldi	McLaren-Ford
German	Nurburgring	03/08/75	C. Reutemann	Brabham-Ford
Austrian	Osterreichring	17/08/75	V. Brambilla	March-Ford
Italian	Monza	07/09/75	C. Regazzoni	Ferrari
U. States	Watkins Glen	05/10/75	N. Lauda	Ferrari

1976

Brazilian	Interlagos	25/01/76	N. Lauda	Ferrari
S. African	Kyalami	06/03/76	N. Lauda	Ferrari
US (West)	Long Beach	28/03/76	C. Regazzoni	Ferrari
Spanish	Jarama	02/05/76	J. Hunt	McLaren-Ford
Belgian	Zolder	16/05/76	N. Lauda	Ferrari
Monaco	Monte Carlo	30/05/76	N. Lauda	Ferrari
Swedish	Anderstorp	13/06/76	J. Scheckter	Tyrrell-Ford
French	Paul Ricard	04/07/76	J. Hunt	McLaren-Ford
British	Brands Hatch	18/07/76	N. Lauda	Ferrari
German	Nurburgring	01/08/76	J. Hunt	McLaren-Ford
Austrian	Osterreichring	15/08/76	J. Watson	Penske-Ford
Dutch	Zandvoort	29/08/76	J. Hunt	McLaren-Ford
Italian	Monza	12/09/76	R. Peterson	March-Ford
Canadian	Mosport Park	03/10/76	J. Hunt	McLaren-Ford
US (East)	Watkins Glen	10/10/76	J. Hunt	McLaren-Ford
Japanese	Fuji	24/10/76	M. Andretti	Lotus-Ford

1977

Argentine	Buenos Aires	09/01/77	J. Scheckter	Wolf-Ford
Brazilian	Interlagos	23/01/77	C. Reutemann	Ferrari
S. African	Kyalami	05/03/77	N. Lauda	Ferrari
US (West)	Long Beach	03/04/77	M. Andretti	Lotus-Ford
Spanish	Jarama	08/05/77	M. Andretti	Lotus-Ford
Monaco	Monte Carlo	22/05/77	J. Scheckter	Wolf-Ford
Belgian	Zolder	05/06/77	G. Nilsson	Lotus-Ford
Swedish	Anderstorp	19/06/77	J. Laffite	Ligier-Matra
French	Dijon	03/07/77	M. Andretti	Lotus-Ford
British	Silverstone	16/07/77	J. Hunt	McLaren-Ford
German	Hockenheim	31/07/77	N. Lauda	Ferrari
Austrian	Osterreichring	14/08/77	A. Jones	Shadow-Ford
Dutch	Zandvoort	28/08/77	N. Lauda	Ferrari
Italian	Monza	11/09/77	M. Andretti	Lotus-Ford
US (East)	Watkins Glen	02/10/77	J. Hunt	McLaren-Ford
Canadian	Mosport Park	09/10/77	J. Scheckter	Wolf-Ford
Japanese	Fuji	23/10/77	J. Hunt	McLaren-Ford

1978

Argentine	Buenos Aires	15/01/78	M. Andretti	Lotus-Ford
Brazilian	Rio de Janeiro	29/01/78	C. Reutemann	Ferrari
S. African	Kyalami	04/03/78	R. Peterson	Lotus-Ford
US (West)	Long Beach	02/04/78	C. Reutemann	Ferrari
Monaco	Monte Carlo	07/05/78	P. Depailler	Tyrrell-Ford
Belgian	Zolder	21/05/78	M. Andretti	Lotus-Ford
Spanish	Jarama	04/06/78	M. Andretti	Lotus-Ford
Swedish	Anderstorp	17/06/78	N. Lauda	Brabham-Alfa
French	Paul Ricard	02/07/78	M. Andretti	Lotus-Ford
British	Brands Hatch	16/07/78	C. Reutemann	Ferrari
German	Hockenheim	30/07/78	M. Andretti	Lotus-Ford
Austrian	Osterreichring	13/08/78	R. Peterson	Lotus-Ford
Dutch	Zandvoort	27/08/78	M. Andretti	Lotus-Ford
Italian	Monza	10/09/78	N. Lauda	Brabham-Alfa
US (East)	Watkins Glen	01/10/78	C. Reutemann	Ferrari
Canadian	Montreal	08/10/78	G. Villeneuve	Ferrari

1979

Argentine	Buenos Aires	21/01/79	J. Laffite	Ligier-Ford
Brazilian	Interlagos	04/02/79	J. Laffite	Ligier-Ford
S. African	Kyalami	03/03/79	G. Villeneuve	Ferrari
US (West)	Long Beach	08/04/79	G. Villeneuve	Ferrari
Spanish	Jarama	29/04/79	P. Depailler	Ligier-Ford
Belgian	Zolder	13/05/79	J. Scheckter	Ferrari
Monaco	Monte Carlo	27/05/79	J. Scheckter	Ferrari
French	Dijon	01/07/79	J.P. Jabouille	Renault
British	Silverstone	14/07/79	C. Regazzoni	Williams-Ford
German	Hockenheim	29/07/79	A. Jones	Williams-Ford
Austrian	Osterreichring	12/08/79	A. Jones	Williams-Ford
Dutch	Zandvoort	26/08/79	A. Jones	Williams-Ford
Italian	Monza	09/09/79	J. Scheckter	Ferrari
Canadian	Montreal	30/09/79	A. Jones	Williams-Ford
US (East)	Watkins Glen	07/10/79	G. Villeneuve	Ferrari

1980

Argentine	Buenos Aires	13/01/80	A. Jones	Williams-Ford
Brazilian	Interlagos	27/01/80	R. Arnoux	Renault
S. African	Kyalami	01/03/80	R. Arnoux	Renault
US (West)	Long Beach	30/03/80	N. Piquet	Brabham-Ford
Belgian	Zolder	04/05/80	D. Pironi	Ligier-Ford
Monaco	Monte Carlo	18/05/80	C. Reutemann	Williams-Ford
French	Paul Ricard	29/06/80	A. Jones	Williams-Ford
British	Brands Hatch	13/07/80	A. Jones	Williams Ford
German	Hockenheim	10/08/80	J. Laffite	Ligier-Ford
Austrian	Osterreichring	17/08/80	J.P. Jabouille	Renault
Dutch	Zandvoort	31/08/80	N. Piquet	Brabham-Ford
Italian	Imola	14/09/80	N. Piquet	Brabham-Ford
Canadian	Montreal	28/09/80	A. Jones	Williams-Ford
US (East)	Watkins Glen	05/10/80	A. Jones	Williams-Ford

1981

US (West)	Long Beach	15/03/81	A. Jones	Williams-Ford
Brazilian	Rio de Janeiro	29/03/81	C. Reutemann	Williams-Ford
Argentine	Buenos Aires	12/04/81	N. Piquet	Brabham-Ford
San Marino	Imola	03/05/81	N. Piquet	Brabham-Ford
Belgian	Zolder	17/05/81	C. Reutemann	Williams-Ford
Monaco	Monte Carlo	31/05/81	G. Villeneuve	Ferrari
Spanish	Jarama	21/06/81	G. Villeneuve	Ferrari
French	Dijon	05/07/81	A. Prost	Renault
British	Silverstone	18/07/81	J. Watson	McLaren-Ford
German	Hockenheim	02/08/81	N. Piquet	Brabham-Ford
Austrian	Osterreichring	16/08/81	J. Laffite	Ligier-Matra
Dutch	Zandvoort	30/08/81	A. Prost	Renault
Italian	Monza	13/09/81	A. Prost	Renault
Canadian	Montreal	27/09/81	J. Laffite	Ligier-Matra
Las Vegas	Caesar's Palace	17/10/81	A. Jones	Williams-Ford

1982

S. African	Kyalami	23/01/82	A. Prost	Renault
Brazilian	Rio de Janeiro	21/03/82	A. Prost	Renault
US (West)	Long Beach	04/04/82	N. Lauda	McLaren-Ford
San Marino	Imola	25/04/82	D. Pironi	Ferrari
Belgian	Zolder	09/05/82	J. Watson	McLaren-Ford
Monaco	Monte Carlo	23/05/82	R. Patrese	Brabham-Ford

Detroit	Detroit	06/06/82	J. Watson	McLaren-Ford
Canadian	Montreal	13/06/82	N. Piquet	Brabham-BMW
Dutch	Zandvoort	03/07/82	D. Pironi	Ferrari
British	Brands Hatch	18/07/82	N. Lauda	McLaren-Ford
French	Paul Ricard	25/07/82	R. Arnoux	Renault
German	Hockenheim	08/08/82	P. Tambay	Ferrari
Austrian	Osterreichring	15/08/82	E. de Angelis	Lotus-Ford
Swiss	Dijon	29/08/82	K. Rosberg	Williams-Ford
Italian	Monza	12/09/82	R. Arnoux	Renault
Las Vegas	Caesar's Palace	25/09/82	M. Alboreto	Tyrrell-Ford

1983

Brazilian	Rio de Janeiro	13/03/83	N. Piquet	Brabham-BMW
US (West)	Long Beach	27/03/83	J. Watson	McLaren-Ford
French	Paul Ricard	17/04/83	A. Prost	Renault
San Marino	Imola	01/05/83	P. Tambay	Ferrari
Monaco	Monte Carlo	15/05/83	K. Rosberg	Williams-Ford
Belgian	Spa	22/05/83	A. Prost	Renault
Detroit	Detroit	05/06/83	M. Alboreto	Tyrrell-Ford
Canadian	Montreal	12/06/83	R. Arnoux	Ferrari
British	Silverstone	16/07/83	A. Prost	Renault
German	Hockenheim	07/08/83	R. Arnoux	Ferrari
Austrian	Osterreichring	14/08/83	A. Prost	Renault
Dutch	Zandvoort	28/08/83	R. Arnoux	Ferrari
Italian	Monza	11/09/83	N. Piquet	Brabham-BMW
European	Brands Hatch	25/09/83	N. Piquet	Brabham-BMW
S. African	Kyalami	16/10/83	R. Patrese	Brabham-BMW

1984

Brazilian	Rio de Janeiro	25/03/84	A. Prost	McLaren-TAG
S. African	Kyalami	07/04/84	N. Lauda	McLaren-TAG
Belgian	Zolder	29/04/84	M. Alboreto	Ferrari
San Marino	Imola	06/05/84	A. Prost	McLaren-TAG
French	Dijon	20/05/84	N. Lauda	McLaren-TAG
Monaco	Monte Carlo	03/06/84	A. Prost	McLaren-TAG
Canadian	Montreal	17/06/84	N. Piquet	Brabham-BMW
Detroit	Detroit	24/06/84	N. Piquet	Brabham-BMW
Dallas	Fir Park	08/07/84	K. Rosberg	Williams-Honda
British	Brands Hatch	22/07/84	N. Lauda	McLaren-TAG
German	Hockenheim	05/08/84	A. Prost	McLaren-TAG
Austrian	Osterreichring	19/08/84	N. Lauda	McLaren-TAG
Dutch	Zandvoort	26/08/84	A. Prost	McLaren-TAG
Italian	Monza	09/09/84	N. Lauda	McLaren-TAG
European	Nurburgring	07/10/84	A. Prost	McLaren-TAG
Portuguese	Estoril	21/10/84	A. Prost	McLaren-TAG

1985

Brazilian	Rio de Janeiro	07/04/85	A. Prost	McLaren-TAG
Portuguese	Estoril	21/04/85	A. Senna	Lotus-Renault
San Marino	Imola	05/05/85	E. de Angelis	Lotus-Renault
Monaco	Monte Carlo	19/05/85	A. Prost	McLaren-TAG
Canadian	Montreal	16/06/85	M. Alboreto	Ferrari
Detroit	Detroit	23/06/85	K. Rosberg	Williams-Honda
French	Paul Ricard	07/07/85	N. Piquet	Brabham-BMW
British	Silverstone	21/07/85	A. Prost	McLaren-TAG
German	Nurburgring	04/08/85	M. Alboreto	Ferrari
Austrian	Osterreichring	18/08/85	A. Prost	McLaren-TAG

Dutch	Zandvoort	25/08/85	N. Lauda	McLaren-TAG
Italian	Monza	08/09/85	A. Prost	McLaren-TAG
Belgian	Spa	15/09/85	A. Senna	Lotus-Renault
European	Brands Hatch	06/10/85	N. Mansell	Williams-Honda
S. African	Kyalami	19/10/85	N. Mansell	Williams-Honda
Australian	Adelaide	03/11/85	K. Rosberg	Williams-Honda

1986

Brazilian	Rio de Janeiro	23/03/86	N. Piquet	Williams-Honda
Spanish	Jerez	13/04/86	A. Senna	Lotus-Renault
San Marino	Imola	27/04/86	A. Prost	McLaren-TAG
Monaco	Monte Carlo	11/05/86	A. Prost	McLaren-TAG
Belgian	Spa	25/05/86	N. Mansell	Williams-Honda
Canadian	Montreal	15/06/86	N. Mansell	Williams-Honda
Detroit	Detroit	22/06/86	A. Senna	Lotus-Renault
French	Paul Ricard	06/07/86	N. Mansell	Williams-Honda
British	Brands Hatch	13/07/86	N. Mansell	Williams-Honda
German	Hockenheim	27/07/86	N. Piquet	Williams-Honda
Hungarian	Hungaroring	10/08/86	N. Piquet	Williams-Honda
Austrian	Osterreichring	17/08/86	A. Prost	McLaren-TAG
Italian	Monza	07/09/86	N. Piquet	Williams-Honda
Portuguese	Estoril	21/09/86	N. Mansell	Williams-Honda
Mexican	Mexico City	12/10/86	G. Berger	Benetton-BMW
Australian	Adelaide	26/10/86	A. Prost	McLaren-TAG

1987

Brazilian	Rio de Janeiro	12/04/87	A. Prost	McLaren-TAG
San Marino	Imola	03/05/87	N. Mansell	Williams-Honda
Belgian	Spa	17/05/87	A. Prost	McLaren-TAG
Monaco	Monte Carlo	31/05/87	A. Senna	Lotus-Honda
U. States	Detroit	21/06/87	A. Senna	Lotus-Honda
French	Paul Ricard	05/07/87	N. Mansell	Williams-Honda
British	Silverstone	12/07/87	N. Mansell	Williams-Honda
German	Hockenheim	26/07/87	N. Piquet	Williams-Honda

Hungarian	Hungaroring	09/08/87	N. Piquet	Williams-Honda
Austrian	Osterreichring	16/08/87	N. Mansell	Williams-Honda
Italian	Monza	06/09/87	N. Piquet	Williams-Honda
Portuguese	Estoril	20/09/87	A. Prost	McLaren-TAG
Spanish	Jerez	27/09/87	N. Mansell	Williams-Honda
Mexican	Mexico City	18/10/87	N. Mansell	Williams-Honda
Japanese	Suzuka	01/11/87	G. Berger	Ferrari
Australian	Adelaide	15/11/87	G. Berger	Ferrari

1988

Brazilian	Rio de Janeiro	03/04/88	A. Prost	McLaren-Honda
San Marino	Imola	01/05/88	A. Senna	McLaren-Honda
Monaco	Monte Carlo	15/05/88	A. Prost	McLaren-Honda
Mexican	Mexico City	29/05/88	A. Prost	McLaren-Honda
Canadian	Montreal	12/06/88	A. Senna	McLaren-Honda
U. States	Detroit	19/06/88	A. Senna	McLaren-Honda
French	Paul Ricard	03/07/88	A. Prost	McLaren-Honda
British	Silverstone	10/07/88	A. Senna	McLaren-Honda
German	Hockenheim	24/07/88	A. Senna	McLaren-Honda
Hungarian	Hungaroring	07/08/88	A. Senna	McLaren-Honda
Belgian	Spa	28/08/88	A. Senna	McLaren-Honda
Italian	Monza	11/09/88	G. Berger	Ferrari
Portuguese	Estoril	25/09/88	A. Prost	McLaren-Honda
Spanish	Jerez	02/10/88	A. Prost	McLaren-Honda
Japanese	Suzuka	30/10/88	A. Senna	McLaren-Honda
Australian	Adelaide	13/11/88	A. Prost	McLaren-Honda

1989

Brazilian	Rio de Janeiro	26/03/89	N. Mansell	Ferrari
San Marino	Imola	23/04/89	A. Senna	McLaren-Honda
Monaco	Monte Carlo	07/05/89	A. Senna	McLaren-Honda
Mexican	Mexico City	28/05/89	A. Senna	McLaren-Honda
U. States	Phoenix	04/06/89	A. Prost	McLaren-Honda
Canadian	Montreal	18/06/89	T. Boutsen	Williams-Renault
French	Paul Ricard	09/07/89	A. Prost	McLaren-Honda
British	Silverstone	16/07/89	A. Prost	McLaren-Honda
German	Hockenheim	30/07/89	A. Senna	McLaren-Honda
Hungarian	Hungaroring	13/08/89	N. Mansell	Ferrari
Belgian	Spa	27/08/89	A. Senna	McLaren-Honda
Italian	Monza	10/09/89	A. Prost	McLaren-Honda
Portuguese	Estoril	24/09/89	G. Berger	Ferrari
Spanish	Jerez	01/10/89	A. Senna	McLaren-Honda
Japanese	Suzuka	22/10/89	A. Nannini	Benetton-Ford
Australian	Adelaide	05/11/89	T. Boutsen	Williams-Renault

1990

U. States	Phoenix	11/03/90	A. Senna	McLaren-Honda
Brazilian	Interlagos	25/03/90	A. Prost	Ferrari
San Marino	Imola	13/05/90	R. Patrese	Williams-Renault
Monaco	Monte Carlo	27/05/90	A. Senna	McLaren-Honda
Canadian	Montreal	10/06/90	A. Senna	McLaren-Honda
Mexican	Mexico City	24/06/90	A. Prost	Ferrari
French	Paul Ricard	08/07/90	A. Prost	Ferrari
British	Silverstone	15/07/90	A. Prost	Ferrari
German	Hockenheim	29/07/90	A. Senna	McLaren-Honda
Hungarian	Hungaroring	12/08/90	T. Boutsen	Williams-Renault
Belgian	Spa	26/08/90	A. Senna	McLaren-Honda
Italian	Monza	09/09/90	A. Senna	McLaren-Honda

Portuguese	Estoril	23/09/90	N. Mansell	Ferrari
Spanish	Jerez	30/09/90	A. Prost	Ferrari
Japanese	Suzuka	21/10/90	N. Piquet	Benetton-Ford
Australian	Adelaide	04/11/90	N. Piquet	Benetton-Ford

1991

U. States	Phoenix	10/03/91	A. Senna	McLaren-Honda
Brazilian	Interlagos	24/03/91	A. Senna	McLaren-Honda
San Marino	Imola	28/04/91	A. Senna	McLaren-Honda
Monaco	Monte Carlo	12/05/91	A. Senna	McLaren-Honda
Canadian	Montreal	02/06/91	N. Piquet	Benetton-Ford
Mexican	Mexico City	16/06/91	R. Patrese	Williams-Renault
French	Magny-Cours	07/07/91	N. Mansell	Williams-Renault
British	Silverstone	14/07/91	N. Mansell	Williams-Renault
German	Hockenheim	28/07/91	N. Mansell	Williams-Renault
Hungarian	Hungaroring	11/08/91	A. Senna	McLaren-Honda
Belgian	Spa	25/08/91	A. Senna	McLaren-Honda
Italian	Monza	08/09/91	N. Mansell	Williams-Renault
Portuguese	Estoril	22/09/91	R. Patrese	Williams-Renault
Spanish	Barcelona	29/09/91	N. Mansell	Williams-Renault
Japanese	Suzuka	20/10/91	G. Berger	McLaren-Honda
Australian	Adelaide	03/11/91	A. Senna	McLaren-Honda

1992

S. African	Kyalami	01/03/92	N. Mansell	Williams-Renault
Mexican	Mexico City	22/03/92	N. Mansell	Williams-Renault
Brazilian	Interlagos	05/04/92	N. Mansell	Williams-Renault
Spanish	Barcelona	03/05/92	N. Mansell	Williams-Renault
San Marino	Imola	17/05/92	N. Mansell	Williams-Renault
Monaco	Monte Carlo	31/05/92	A. Senna	McLaren-Honda
Canadian	Montreal	14/06/92	G. Berger	McLaren-Honda
French	Magny-Cours	05/07/92	N. Mansell	Williams-Renault
British	Silverstone	12/07/92	N. Mansell	Williams-Renault
German	Hockenheim	26/07/92	N. Mansell	Williams-Renault
Hungarian	Hungaroring	16/08/92	A. Senna	McLaren-Honda
Belgian	Spa	30/08/92	M. Schumacher	Benetton-Ford
Italian	Monza	13/09/92	A. Senna	McLaren-Honda
Portuguese	Estoril	27/09/92	N. Mansell	Williams-Renault
Japanese	Suzuka	25/10/92	R. Patrese	Williams-Renault
Australian	Adelaide	08/11/92	G. Berger	McLaren-Honda

1993

S. African	Kyalami	14/03/93	A. Prost	Wiiliams-Renault
Brazilian	Interlagos	28/03/93	A. Senna	McLaren-Ford
European	Donington	11/04/93	A. Senna	McLaren-Ford
San Marino	Imola	25/04/93	A. Prost	Williams-Renault
Spanish	Barcelona	09/05/93	A. Prost	Williams-Renault
Monaco	Monte Carlo	23/05/93	A. Senna	McLaren-Ford
Canadian	Montreal	13/06/93	A. Prost	Williams-Renault
French	Magny-Cours	04/07/93	A. Prost	Williams-Renault
British	Silverstone	11/07/93	A. Prost	Williams-Renault
German	Hockenheim	25/07/93	A. Prost	Williams-Renault
Hungarian	Hungaroring	15/08/93	D. Hill	Williams-Renault
Belgian	Spa	29/08/93	D. Hill	Williams-Renault
Italian	Monza	12/09/93	D. Hill	Williams-Renault
Portuguese	Estoril	26/09/93	M. Schumacher	Benetton-Ford
Japanese	Suzuka	24/10/93	A. Senna	McLaren-Ford
Australian	Adelaide	07/11/93	A. Senna	McLaren-Ford

1994

Brazilian	Interlagos	27/03/94	M. Schumacher	Benetton-Ford
Pacific	Aida	17/04/94	M. Schumacher	Benetton-Ford
San Marino	Imola	01/05/94	M. Schumacher	Benetton-Ford
Monaco	Monte Carlo	15/05/94	M. Schumacher	Benetton-Ford
Spanish	Barcelona	29/05/94	D. Hill	Williams-Renault
Canadian	Montreal	21/06/94	M.Schumacher	Benetton-Ford
French	Magny-Cours	03/07/94	M. Schumacher	Benetton-Ford
British	Silverstone	10/07/94	D. Hill	Williams-Renault
German	Hockenheim	31/07/94	G. Berger	Ferrari
Hungarian	Hungaroring	14/08/94	M. Schumacher	Benetton-Ford
Belgian	Spa	28/08/94	D. Hill	Williams-Renault
Italian	Monza	11/09/94	D. Hill	Williams-Renault
Portuguese	Estoril	25/09/94	D. Hill	Williams-Renault
European	Jerez	16/10/94	M. Schumacher	Benetton-Ford
Japanese	Suzuka	06/11/94	D. Hill	Williams-Renault
Australian	Adelaide	13/11/94	N. Mansell	Williams-Renault

INDIANAPOLIS 500 WINNERS
1950-1960

30/05/50	J. Parsons	Wynn's Friction Proofing
29/05/51	L. Wallard	Belanger
30/05/52	T. Ruttman	Agajanian
30/05/53	B. Vukovich	Fuel Injection
31/05/54	B. Vukovich	Fuel Injection
30/05/55	B. Sweikert	John Zink
30/05/56	P. Flaherty	John Zink
30/05/57	S. Hanks	Belond Exhaust
30/05/58	J. Bryan	Belond Exhaust
30/05/59	R. Ward	Leader Card
30/05/60	J. Rathmann	Ken-Paul

DRIVERS' WORLD CHAMPIONSHIP 1950-1994

Driver-Nationality	Races	Wins	Points	
1950				
1 Nino Farina - Italy	6	3	30	
2 Juan Manuel Fangio - Argentina	6	3	27	
3 Luigi Fagioli - Italy	6	0	24	(28)
4 Louis Rosier - France	6	0	13	
5 Alberto Ascari - Italy	4	0	11	
6 Johnnie Parsons - United States	1*	1	8	
1951				
1 Juan Manuel Fangio - Argentina	7	3	31	(37)
2 Alberto Ascari - Italy	7	2	25	(28)
3 Jose Froilan Gonzalez - Argentina	6	1	24	(27)
4 Nino Farina - Italy	7	1	19	(22)
5 Luigi Villoresi - Italy	7	0	15	(18)
6 Piero Taruffi - Italy	5	0	10	
1952				
1 Alberto Ascari - Italy	7*	6	36	(53.5)
2 Nino Farina - Italy	7	0	24	(27)
3 Piero Taruffi - Italy	6	1	22	
4= Rudi Fischer - Switzerland	5	0	10	
Mike Hawthorn - Great Britain	5	0	10	
6 Robert Manzon - France	7	0	9	
1953				
1 Alberto Ascari - Italy	8	5	34.5	(47)
2 Juan Manuel Fangio - Argentina	8	1	27.5	(29)
3 Nino Farina - Italy	8	1	26	(32)
4 Mike Hawthorn - Great Britain	8	1	19	(27)
5 Luigi Villoresi - Italy	8	0	17	
6 Jose Froilan Gonzalez - Argentina	5	0	13.5	(14.5)
1954				
1 Juan Manuel Fangio - Argentina	8	6	42	(57.14)
2 Jose Froilan Gonzalez - Argentina	7	1	25.14	(26.64)
3 Mike Hawthorn - Great Britain	8	1	24.64	
4 Maurice Trintignant - France	8	0	17	
5 Karl Kling - Germany	6	0	12	
6= Hans Herrmann - Germany	5	0	8	
Bill Vukovich - United States	1*	1	8	
1955				
1 Juan Manuel Fangio - Argentina	6	4	40	(41)
2 Stirling Moss - Great Britain	6	1	23	
3 Eugenio Castellotti - Italy	6	0	12	

4	Maurice Trintignant - France	6	1	11.33	
5	Nino Farina - Italy	3	0	10.33	
6	Piero Taruffi - Italy	3	0	9	

1956

1	Juan Manuel Fangio - Argentina	7	3	30	(33)
2	Stirling Moss - Great Britain	7	2	27	(28)
3	Peter Collins - Great Britain	7	2	25	
4	Jean Behra - France	7	0	22	
5	Pat Flaherty - United States	1*	1	8	
6	Eugenio Castellotti - Italy	7	0	7.5	

1957

1	Juan Manuel Fangio - Argentina	7	4	40	(46)
2	Stirling Moss - Great Britain	6	3	25	
3	Luigi Musso - Italy	6	0	16	
4	Mike Hawthorn - Great Britain	6	0	13	
5	Tony Brooks - Great Britain	5	1	11	
6	Masten Gregory - United States	4	0	10	

1958

1	Mike Hawthorn - Great Britain	10	1	42	(49)
2	Stirling Moss - Great Britain	10	4	41	
3	Tony Brooks - Great Britain	9	3	24	
4	Roy Salvadori - Great Britain	9	0	15	
5=	Peter Collins - Great Britain	7	1	14	
	Harry Schell - United States	10	0	14	

1959

1	Jack Brabham - Australia	8	2	31	(34)
2	Tony Brooks - Great Britain	8	2	27	
3	Stirling Moss - Great Britain	8	2	25.5	
4	Phil Hill - United States	7	0	20	
5	Maurice Trintignant - France	8	0	19	
6	Bruce McLaren - New Zealand	7	1	16.5	

1960

1	Jack Brabham - Australia	8	5	43	
2	Bruce McLaren - New Zealand	8	1	34	(37)
3	Stirling Moss - Great Britain	5	2	19	
4	Innes Ireland - Great Britain	8	0	18	
5	Phil Hill - United States	9	1	16	
6=	Olivier Gendebien - Belgium	5	0	10	
	Wolfgang von Trips - Germany	9	0	10	

1961

1	Phil Hill - United States	7	2	34	(38)
2	Wolfgang von Trips - Germany	7	2	33	
3=	Dan Gurney - United States	8	0	21	
	Stirling Moss - Great Britain	8	2	21	
4	Richie Ginther - United States	7	0	16	
5	Innes Ireland - Great Britain	6	1	12	

1962

1	Graham Hill - Great Britain	9	4	42	(52)
2	Jim Clark - Great Britain	9	3	30	
3	Bruce McLaren - New Zealand	9	1	27	(32)
4	John Surtees - Great Britain	9	0	19	
5	Dan Gurney - United States	7	1	15	
6	Phil Hill - United States	6	0	14	

1963

1	Jim Clark - Great Britain	10	7	54	(73)
2	Graham Hill - Great Britain	10	2	29	
3	Richie Ginther - United States	10	0	29	(34)
4	John Surtees - Great Britain	10	1	22	
5	Dan Gurney - United States	10	0	19	
6	Bruce McLaren - New Zealand	10	0	17	

1964

1	John Surtees - Great Britain	10	2	40	
2	Graham Hill - Great Britain	10	1	39	(41)
3	Jim Clark - Great Britain	10	3	32	
4=	Lorenzo Bandini - Italy	10	1	23	
	Richie Ginther - United States	10	0	23	
5	Dan Gurney - United States	10	2	19	

1965

1	Jim Clark - Great Britain	9	6	54	
2	Graham Hill - Great Britain	10	2	40	(47)
3	Jackie Stewart - Great Britain	10	1	33	(34)
4	Dan Gurney - United States	9	0	25	
5	John Surtees - Great Britain	8	0	17	
6	Lorenzo Bandini - Italy	10	0	13	

1966

1	Jack Brabham - Australia	9	4	42	(45)
2	John Surtees - Great Britain	9	2	28	
3	Jochen Rindt - Austria	9	0	22	(24)
4	Denny Hulme - New Zealand	9	0	18	
5	Graham Hill - Great Britain	9	0	17	
6	Jim Clark - Great Britain	8	1	16	

1967

1	Denny Hulme - New Zealand	11	2	51	
2	Jack Brabham - Australia	11	2	46	(48)
3	Jim Clark - Great Britain	11	4	41	
4=	Chris Amon - New Zealand	10	0	20	
	John Surtees - Great Britain	9	1	20	
5=	Graham Hill - Great Britain	11	0	15	
	Pedro Rodriguez - Mexico	8	1	15	

1968

1	Graham Hill - Great Britain	12	3	48	
2	Jackie Stewart - Great Britain	10	3	36	
3	Denny Hulme - New Zealand	12	2	33	

4	Jacky Ickx - Belgium	9	1	27
5	Bruce McLaren - New Zealand	11	1	22
6	Pedro Rodriguez - Mexico	12	0	18

1969

1	Jackie Stewart - Great Britain	11	6	63
2	Jacky Ickx - Belgium	11	2	37
3	Bruce McLaren - New Zealand	10	0	26
4	Jochen Rindt - Austria	10	1	22
5	Jean-Pierre Beltoise - France	11	0	21
6	Denny Hulme - New Zealand	11	1	20

1970

1	Jochen Rindt - Austria	9	5	45
2	Jacky Ickx - Belgium	13	3	40
3	Clay Regazzoni - Switzerland	8	1	33
4	Denny Hulme - New Zealand	11	0	27
5=	Jack Brabham - Australia	13	1	25
	Jackie Stewart - Great Britain	13	1	25

1971

1	Jackie Stewart - Great Britain	11	6	62
2	Ronnie Peterson - Sweden	11	0	33
3	Francois Cevert - France	11	1	26
4=	Jacky Ickx - Belgium	11	1	19
	Jo Siffert - Switzerland	11	1	19
6	Emerson Fittipaldi - Brazil	10	0	16

1972

1	Emerson Fittipaldi - Brazil	12	5	61
2	Jackie Stewart - Great Britain	11	4	45
3	Denny Hulme - New Zealand	12	1	39
4	Jacky Ickx - Belgium	12	1	27
5	Peter Revson - United States	9	0	23
6=	Francois Cevert - France	12	0	15
	Clay Regazzoni - Switzerland	10	0	15

1973

1	Jackie Stewart - Great Britain	14	5	71
2	Emerson Fittipaldi - Brazil	15	3	55
3	Ronnie Peterson - Sweden	15	4	52
4	Francois Cevert - France	14	0	47
5	Peter Revson - United States	14	2	38
6	Denny Hulme - New Zealand	15	1	26

1974

1	Emerson Fittipaldi - Brazil	15	3	55
2	Clay Regazzoni - Switzerland	15	1	52
3	Jody Scheckter - South Africa	15	2	45
4	Niki Lauda - Austria	15	2	38
5	Ronnie Peterson - Sweden	15	3	35
6	Carlos Reutemann - Argentina	15	3	32

1975

1	Niki Lauda - Austria	14	5	64.5
2	Emerson Fittipaldi - Brazil	13	2	45
3	Carlos Reutemann - Argentina	14	1	37
4	James Hunt - Great Britain	14	1	33
5	Clay Regazzoni - Switzerland	14	1	25
6	Carlos Pace - Brazil	14	1	24

1976

1	James Hunt - Great Britain	16	6	69
2	Niki Lauda - Austria	14	5	68
3	Jody Scheckter - South Africa	16	1	49
4	Patrick Depailler - France	16	0	39
5	Clay Regazzoni - Switzerland	15	1	31
6	Mario Andretti - United States	15	1	22

1977

1	Niki Lauda - Austria	14	3	72
2	Jody Scheckter - South Africa	17	3	55
3	Mario Andretti - United States	17	4	47
4	Carlos Reutemann - Argentina	17	1	42
5	James Hunt - Great Britain	17	3	40
6	Jochen Mass - Germany	17	0	25

Damon Hill and Niki Lauda, Formula 1 Champion 1975, 1977 and 1984, Monaco Grand Prix 1994

1978

1	Mario Andretti - United States	16	6	64
2	Ronnie Peterson - Sweden	14	2	51
3	Carlos Reutemann - Argentina	16	4	48
4	Niki Lauda - Austria	16	2	44
5	Patrick Depailler - France	16	1	34
6	John Watson - Great Britain	16	0	25

1979

1	Jody Scheckter - South Africa	15	3	51	(60)
2	Gilles Villeneuve - Canada	15	3	47	(53)
3	Alan Jones - Australia	15	4	40	(43)
4	Jacques Laffite - France	15	2	36	
5	Clay Regazzoni - Switzerland	15	1	29	(32)
6=	Patrick Depailler - France	7	1	20	(22)
	Carlos Reutemann - Argentina	15	0	20	(25)

1980

1	Alan Jones - Australia	14	5	67	(71)
2	Nelson Piquet - Brazil	14	3	54	
3	Carlos Reutemann - Argentina	14	1	42	(49)
4	Jacques Laffite - France	14	1	34	
5	Didier Pironi - France	14	1	32	
6	Rene Arnoux - France	14	2	29	

1981

1	Nelson Piquet - Brazil	15	3	50
2	Carlos Reutemann - Argentina	15	2	49
3	Alan Jones - Australia	15	2	46
4	Jacques Laffite - France	15	2	44
5	Alain Prost - France	15	3	43
6	John Watson - Great Britain	15	1	27

1982

1	Keke Rosberg - Finland	15	1	44
2=	Didier Pironi - France	10	2	39
	John Watson - Great Britain	15	2	39
4	Alain Prost - Great Britain	16	2	34
5	Niki Lauda - Austria	14	2	30
6	Rene Arnoux - France	16	2	28

1983

1	Nelson Piquet - Brazil	15	3	59
2	Alain Prost - France	15	4	57
3	Rene Arnoux - France	15	3	49
4	Patrick Tambay - France	15	1	40
5	Keke Rosberg - Finland	15	1	27
6=	Eddie Cheever - United States	15	0	22
	John Watson - Great Britain	14	1	22

1984

1	Niki Lauda - Austria	16	5	72
2	Alain Prost - France	16	7	71.5

3	Elio de Angelis - Italy	16	0	34	
4	Michele Alboreto - Italy	16	1	30.5	
5	Nelson Piquet - Brazil	16	2	29	
6	Rene Arnoux - France	16	0	27	

1985

1	Alain Prost - France	16	5	73	(76)
2	Michele Alboreto - Italy	16	2	53	
3	Keke Rosberg - Finland	16	2	40	
4	Ayrton Senna - Brazil	16	2	38	
5	Elio de Angelis - Italy	16	1	33	
6	Nigel Mansell - Great Britain	15	2	31	

1986

1	Alain Prost - France	16	4	72	(74)
2	Nigel Mansell - Great Britain	16	5	70	(72)
3	Nelson Piquet - Brazil	16	4	69	
4	Ayrton Senna - Brazil	16	2	55	
5	Stefan Johansson - Sweden	16	0	23	
6	Keke Rosberg - Finland	16	0	22	

1987

1	Nelson Piquet - Brazil	15	3	73	(76)
2	Nigel Mansell - Great Britain	14	6	61	
3	Ayrton Senna - Brazil	16	2	57	
4	Alain Prost - France	16	3	46	
5	Gerhard Berger - Austria	16	2	36	
6	Stefan Johansson - Sweden	16	0	30	

1988

1	Ayrton Senna - Brazil	16	8	90	(94)
2	Alain Prost - France	16	7	87	(105)
3	Gerhard Berger - Austria	16	1	41	
4	Thierry Boutsen - Belgium	16	0	27	
5	Michele Alboreto - Italy	16	0	24	
6	Nelson Piquet - Brazil	16	0	22	

1989

1	Alain Prost - France	16	4	76	(81)
2	Ayrton Senna - Brazil	16	6	60	
3	Riccardo Patrese - Italy	16	0	40	
4	Nigel Mansell - Great Britain	15	2	38	
5	Thierry Boutsen - Belgium	16	2	37	
6	Alessandro Nannini - Italy	16	1	32	

1990

1	Ayrton Senna - Brazil	16	6	78	
2	Alain Prost - France	16	5	73	
3	Nelson Piquet - Brazil	16	2	44	
4	Gerhard Berger - Austria	16	0	43	
5	Nigel Mansell - Great Britain	16	1	37	
6	Thierry Boutsen - Belgium	16	1	34	

1991

1	Ayrton Senna - Brazil	16	7	96
2	Nigel Mansell - Great Britain	16	5	72
3	Riccardo Patrese - Italy	16	2	53
4	Gerhard Berger - Austria	16	1	43
5	Alain Prost - France	14	0	34
6	Nelson Piquet - Brazil	16	1	26.5

Ayrton Senna

1992

1	Nigel Mansell - Great Britain	16	9	108
2	Riccardo Patrese - Italy	16	1	56
3	Michael Schumacher - Germany	16	1	53
4	Ayrton Senna - Brazil	16	3	50
5	Gerhard Berger - Austria	16	2	49
6	Martin Brundle - Great Britain	16	0	38

1993

1	Alain Prost - France	16	7	99
2	Ayrton Senna - Brazil	16	5	73
3	Damon Hill - Great Britain	16	3	69
4	Michael Schumacher - Germany	16	1	52
5	Riccardo Patrese - Italy	16	0	20
6	Jean Alesi - France	16	0	16

1994

1	Michael Schumacher - Germany	14	8	92
2	Damon Hill - Great Britain	16	6	91
3	Gerhard Berger - Austria	16	1	41
4	Mika Hakkinen - Finland	15	0	26
5	Jean Alesi - France	14	0	24
6	Rubens Barrichello - Brazil	15	0	19

* Includes one drive in the Indianapolis 500

GRAND PRIX POINTS SCORERS 1950-1994

Driver	Nat	Races	Wins	P/P	Points
Andrea de Adamich	It	30	0	0	6
Michele Alboreto	It	194	5	2	186.5
Jean Alesi	Fr	85	0	1	100
Philippe Alliot	Fr	109	0	0	7
Cliff Allison	GB	16	0	0	11
Chris Amon	NZ	96	0	5	83
Bob Anderson	GB	25	0	0	8
Mario Andretti	US	128	12	18	180
Michael Andretti	US	13	0	0	7
Elio de Angelis	It	108	2	3	122
Rene Arnoux	Fr	149	7	18	181
Peter Arundell	GB	11	0	0	12
Alberto Ascari*	It	31	13	14	140.64
Richard Attwood	GB	17	0	0	11
Giancarlo Baghetti	It	21	1	0	14
Julian Bailey	GB	7	0	0	1
Mauro Baldi	It	36	0	0	5
Lorenzo Bandini	It	42	1	1	58
Fabrizio Barbazza	It	8	0	0	2
Rubens Barrichello	Bra	31	0	1	21
Elie Bayol	Fr	7	0	0	2
Carel Godin de Beaufort	Hol	28	0	0	4
Jean Behra	Fr	52	0	0	53.14
Derek Bell	GB	9	0	0	1
Stefan Bellof	Ger	20	0	0	4
Jean-Pierre Beltoise	Fr	86	1	0	77
Gerhard Berger	Aus	163	9	10	306
Eric Bernard	Fra	45	0	0	10
Lucien Bianchi	Bel	17	0	0	6
B. Bira	Thai	19	0	0	8
Mark Blundell	GB	46	0	0	19
Bob Bondurant	US	9	0	0	3
Felice Bonetto	It	15	0	0	17.5
Joakim Bonnier	Swe	104	1	1	39
Slim Borgudd	Swe	10	0	0	1
Thierry Boutsen	Bel	163	3	1	132
Jack Brabham	Aust	126	14	13	261
Vittorio Brambilla	It	74	1	1	15.5
Tony Brise	GB	10	0	0	1
Tony Brooks	GB	38	6	3	75
Alan Brown	GB	8	0	0	2
Martin Brundle	GB	131	0	0	83
Ronnie Bucknum	US	11	0	0	2
Giulio Cabianca	It	3	0	0	3
Alex Caffi	It	56	0	0	6
Ivan Capelli	It	93	0	0	31
Eugenio Castellotti	It	14	0	1	19.5
Johnny Cecotto	Ven	18	0	0	1
Andrea de Cesaris	It	208	0	1	59
Francois Cevert	Fr	47	1	0	89
Eugene Chaboud	Fr	3	0	0	1

Eddie Cheever	US	132	0	0	70
Louis Chiron	Mon	15	0	0	4
Jim Clark	GB	72	25	33	274
Peter Collins	GB	32	3	0/1+	47
Erik Comas	Fr	59	0	0	7
David Coulthard	GB	8	0	0	14
Piers Courage	GB	28	0	0	20
Derek Daly	Ire	49	0	0	15
Christian Danner	Ger	36	0	0	4
Patrick Depailler	Fr	95	2	1	141
Mark Donohue	US	14	0	0	8
Johnny Dumfries	GB	15	0	0	3
Vic Elford	GB	13	0	0	8
Philippe Etancelin	Fr	12	0	0	3
Teo Fabi	It	64	0	3	23
Luigi Fagioli	It	7	1	0	32
Jack Fairman	GB	12	0	0	5
Juan Manuel Fangio	Arg	51	24	28/29+	277.14
Giuseppe Farina	It	33	5	5	127.33
Rudi Fischer	Swi	7	0	0	10
Christian Fittipaldi	Bra	40	0	0	12
Emerson Fittipaldi	Bra	144	14	6	281
Wilson Fittipaldi	Bra	36	0	0	3
Ron Flockhart	GB	13	0	0	5
George Follmer	US	12	0	0	5
Heinz-Harald Frentzen	Ger	15	0	0	7
Paul Frere	Bel	11	0	0	11
Bertrand Gachot	Fr	36	0	0	5
Oscar Galvez	Arg	1	0	0	2
Howden Ganley	NZ	35	0	0	10
Olivier Gendebien	Bel	14	0	0	18
Gerino Gerini	It	6	0	0	1.5
Peter Gethin	GB	30	1	0	11
Piercarlo Ghinzani	It	76	0	0	2
Bruno Giacomelli	It	69	0	1	14
Richie Ginther	US	52	1	0	107
Yves Giraud-Cabantous	Fr	13	0	0	5
Ignazio Giunti	It	4	0	0	3
Francisco Godia	Sp	13	0	0	6
Jose Froilan Gonzalez	Arg	26	2	3	77.64
Horace Gould	GB	14	0	0	2
Emmanuel de Graffenried	Swi	22	0	0	9
Masten Gregory	US	38	0	0	21
Oliver Grouillard	Fr	41	0	0	1
Mauricio Gugelmin	Bra	74	0	0	10
Dan Gurney	US	86	4	3	133
Mike Hailwood	GB	50	0	0	29
Mika Hakkinen	Fin	48	0	0	43
Jim Hall	US	11	0	0	3
Walt Hansgen	US	2	0	0	2
Mike Hawthorn	GB	45	3	4	127.64
Johnny Herbert	GB	63	0	0	18
Hans Herrmann	Ger	18	0	0	10
Damon Hill	GB	34	9	4	160
Graham Hill	GB	176	14	13	289

Phil Hill	US	48	3	6	98
Denny Hulme	NZ	112	8	1	248
James Hunt	GB	92	10	14	179
Jacky Ickx	Bel	116	8	13	181
Innes Ireland	GB	50	1	0	47
Eddie Irvine	GB	15	0	0	7
Chris Irwin	GB	10	0	0	2
Jean-Pierre Jabouille	Fr	49	2	6	21
Jean-Pierre Jarier	Fr	136	0	3	31.5
Stefan Johansson	Swe	79	0	0	88
Alan Jones	Aust	116	12	6	206
Ukyo Katayama	Jap	46	0	0	5
Karl Kling	Ger	11	0	0	17
Jacques Laffite	Fr	176	6	7	228
Chico Landi	Bra	6	0	0	1.5
Hermann Lang	Ger	2	0	0	2
Nicola Larini	It	44	0	0	6
Niki Lauda	Aus	171	25	24	420.5
Neville Lederle	SA	1	0	0	1
J.J. Lehto	Fin	62	0	0	10
Gijs van Lennep	Hol	8	0	0	2
Jack Lewis	GB	9	0	0	3
Stuart Lewis-Evans	GB	14	0	2	16
Guy Ligier	Fr	12	0	0	1
Lella Lombardi	It	12	0	0	0.5
John Love	Zim	9	0	0	6
Tony Maggs	SA	25	0	0	26
Umberto Maglioli	It	10	0	0	3.33
Willy Mairesse	Bel	12	0	0	7
Nigel Mansell	GB	185	31	32	482
Sergio Mantovani	It	7	0	0	4
Robert Manzon	Fr	28	0	0	16
Onofre Marimon	Arg	11	0	0	8.14
Pierluigi Martini	It	110	0	0	18
Jochen Mass	Ger	105	1	0	71
Bruce McLaren	NZ	103	4	0	196.5
Carlos Menditeguy	Arg	10	0	0	9
Arturo Merzario	It	57	0	0	11
Roberto Mieres	Arg	17	0	0	13
John Miles	GB	12	0	0	2
Gerhard Mitter	Ger	5	0	0	3
Stefano Modena	It	70	0	0	17
Gianni Morbidelli	It	50	0	0	3.5
Roberto Moreno	Bra	25	0	0	15
Silvio Moser	Swi	12	0	0	3
Stirling Moss	GB	66	16	16	186.64
Luigi Musso	It	24	1	0	44
Satoru Nakajima	Jap	74	0	0	16
Alessandro Nannini	It	77	1	0	65
Gunnar Nilsson	Swe	31	1	0	31
Jackie Oliver	GB	50	0	0	13
Carlos Pace	Bra	72	1	1	58
Jonathan Palmer	GB	82	0	0	14
Olivier Panis	Fra	16	0	0	9
Mike Parkes	GB	6	0	1	14
Reg Parnell	GB	6	0	0	9
Riccardo Patrese	It	256	6	8	281

Cesare Perdisa	It	7	0	0	5
Henri Pescarolo	Fr	57	0	0	12
Ronnie Peterson	Swe	123	10	14	206
Nelson Piquet	Bra	204	23	24	485.5
Didier Pironi	Fr	70	3	4	101
Emanuele Pirro	It	37	0	0	3
Dennis Poore	GB	2	0	0	3
Alfonso de Portago	Sp	5	0	0	4
Alain Prost	Fr	199	51	32	798.5
Tom Pryce	GB	42	0	1	19
Nano da Silva Ramos	Bra	7	0	0	2
Hector Rebaque	Mex	41	0	0	13
Brian Redman	GB	12	0	0	8
Clay Regazzoni	Swi	132	5	5	212
Carlos Reutemann	Arg	146	12	6	310
Peter Revson	US	30	2	1	61
Jochen Rindt	Aus	60	6	10	109
Pedro Rodriguez	Mex	55	2	0	71
Ricardo Rodriguez	Mex	5	0	0	4
Keke Rosberg	Fin	114	5	5	159.5
Louis Rosier	Fr	38	0	0	18
Luis Sala	Sp	26	0	0	1
Eliseo Salazar	Ch	24	0	0	3
Roy Salvadori	GB	47	0	0	19
Consalvo Sanesi	It	5	0	0	3
Ludovico Scarfiotti	It	10	1	0	17
Giorgio Scarlatti	It	12	0	0	1
Jody Scheckter	SA	112	10	3	255
Harry Schell	US	56	0	0	30
Tim Schenken	Aust	34	0	0	7
Michael Schumacher	Ger	52	10	6	201
Ayrton Senna	Bra	161	41	65	614
Dorino Serafini	It	1	0	0	3
Chico Serra	Bra	18	0	0	1
Johnny Servoz-Gavin	Fr	12	0	0	9
Jo Siffert	Swi	96	2	2	68
Raymond Sommer	Fr	5	0	0	3
Mike Spence	GB	36	0	0	27
Jackie Stewart	GB	99	27	17	360
Rolf Stommelen	Ger	54	0	0	14
Philippe Streiff	Fr	54	0	0	11
Hans-Joachim Stuck	Ger	74	0	0	29
Danny Sullivan	US	15	0	0	2
Marc Surer	Swi	82	0	0	17
John Surtees	GB	111	6	8	180
Aguri Suzuki	Jap	59	0	0	7
Patrick Tambay	Fr	114	2	5	103
Gabriele Tarquini	It	37	0	0	1
Piero Taruffi	It	18	1	0	41
Henry Taylor	GB	8	0	0	3
John Taylor	GB	5	0	0	1
Trevor Taylor	GB	27	0	0	8
Eric Thompson	GB	1	0	0	2
Maurice Trintignant	Fr	82	2	0	72.33
Wolfgang von Trips	Ger	27	2	1	56
Jos Verstappen	Hol	10	0	0	10

Gilles Villeneuve	Can	67	6	2	107
Luigi Villoresi	It	31	0	0	49
Derek Warwick	GB	147	0	0	71
John Watson	GB	152	5	2	169
Karl Wendlinger	Aus	35	0	0	14
Ken Wharton	GB	15	0	0	3
Peter Whitehead	GB	10	0	0	4
Manfred Winkelhock	Ger	47	0	0	2
Reine Wisell	Swe	22	0	0	13
Alessandro Zanardi	It	25	0	0	1
Renzo Zorzi	It	7	0	0	1

* Does not include one Indianapolis 500 appearance.
+ Peter Collins was given pole position in error, Juan Manuel Fangio actually recorded the fastest lap.

INDIANAPOLIS 500 POINTS
SCORERS 1950-60

Freddie Agabashian	US	8	0	1	1.5
George Amick	US	1	0	0	6
Manny Ayulo	US	4	0	0	2
Bobby Ball	US	2	0	0	2
Tony Bettenhausen	US	11	0	0	11
Johnny Boyd	US	6	0	0	4
Don Branson	US	2	0	0	3
Jimmy Bryan	US	9	1	0	18
Duane Carter	US	8	0	0	6.5
Joie Chitwood	US	1	0	0	1
Art Cross	US	4	0	0	8
Jimmy Davies	US	5	0	0	4
Walt Faulkner	US	5	0	1	1
Pat Flaherty	US	6	1	1	8
Don Freeland	US	8	0	0	4
Paul Goldsmith	US	3	0	0	6
Cecil Green	US	2	0	0	3
Sam Hanks	US	8	1	0	20
Bill Holland	US	2	0	0	6
Bill Homeier	US	3	0	0	1
Eddie Johnson	US	9	0	0	1
Andy Linden	US	7	0	0	5
Jack McGrath	US	6	0	1	9
Mike Nazaruk	US	3	0	0	8
Johnnie Parsons	US	9	1	0	11
Dick Rathmann	US	5	0	1	2
Jim Rathmann	US	10	1	0	29
Mauri Rose	US	2	0	0	4
Paul Russo	US	8	0	0	8.5
Troy Ruttman	US	8	1	0	9.5
Bob Sweikert	US	5	1	0	8
Johnny Thomson	US	8	0	1	10
Bill Vukovich	US	5	2	1	19
Lee Wallard	US	2	1	0	9
Rodger Ward*	US	10	1	0	14

* Does not include two Grand Prix appearances.

MOST GRAND PRIX VICTORIES

Alain Prost	Fr	51
Ayrton Senna	Bra	41
Nigel Mansell	GB	31
Jackie Stewart	GB	27
Jim Clark	GB	25
Niki Lauda	Aus	25
Juan Manuel Fangio	Arg	24+
Nelson Piquet	Bra	23
Stirling Moss	GB	16*
Jack Brabham	Aust	14
Emerson Fittipaldi	Bra	14
Graham Hill	GB	14
Alberto Ascari	It	13
Mario Andretti	US	12
Alan Jones	Aust	12
Carlos Reutemann	Arg	12
James Hunt	GB	10
Ronnie Peterson	Swe	10
Jody Scheckter	SA	10
Michael Schumacher	Ger	10
Gerhard Berger	Aus	9
Damon Hill	GB	9
Denny Hulme	NZ	8
Jacky Ickx	Bel	8
Rene Arnoux	Fr	7
Tony Brooks	GB	6*
Jacques Laffite	Fr	6
Riccardo Patrese	It	6
Jochen Rindt	Aus	6
John Surtees	GB	6
Gilles Villeneuve	Can	6
Michele Alboreto	It	5
Giuseppe Farina	It	5
Clay Regazzoni	Swi	5
Keke Rosberg	Fin	5
John Watson	GB	5
Dan Gurney	US	4
Bruce McLaren	NZ	4
Thierry Boutsen	Bel	3
Peter Collins	GB	3
Mike Hawthorn	GB	3
Phil Hill	US	3
Didier Pironi	Fr	3
Elio de Angelis	It	2
Patrick Depailler	Fr	2
Jose Froilan Gonzalez	Arg	2

Jean-Pierre Jabouille	Fr	2
Peter Revson	US	2
Pedro Rodriguez	Mex	2
Jo Siffert	Swi	2
Patrick Tambay	Fr	2
Maurice Trintignant	Fr	2
Wolfgang von Trips	Ger	2
Giancarlo Baghetti	It	1
Lorenzo Bandini	It	1
Jean-Pierre Beltoise	Fr	1
Joakim Bonnier	Swe	1
Vittorio Brambilla	It	1
Francois Cevert	Fr	1
Luigi Fagioli	It	1*
Peter Gethin	GB	1
Richie Ginther	US	1
Innes Ireland	GB	1
Jochen Mass	Ger	1
Luigi Musso	It	1*
Alessandro Nannini	It	1
Gunnar Nilsson	Swe	1
Carlos Pace	Bra	1
Ludovico Scarfiotti	It	1
Piero Taruffi	It	1

+ Includes two shared victories
* Includes one shared victory

INDIANAPOLIS 500 VICTORIES
1950-1960

Bill Vukovich	US	2
Jimmy Bryan	US	1
Pat Flaherty	US	1
Sam Hanks	US	1
Johnnie Parsons	US	1
Jim Rathmann	US	1
Troy Ruttmann	US	1
Bob Sweikert	US	1
Lee Wallard	US	1
Rodger Ward	US	1

MOST GRAND PRIX
APPEARANCES 1950-1994

Riccardo Patrese	It	256
Andrea de Cesaris	It	208
Nelson Piquet	Bra	204
Alain Prost	Fr	199
Michele Alboreto	It	194
Nigel Mansell	GB	185
Graham Hill	GB	176
Jacques Laffite	Fr	176
Niki Lauda	Aus	171
Gerhard Berger	Aus	163
Thierry Boutsen	Bel	163
Ayrton Senna	Bra	161
John Watson	GB	152
Rene Arnoux	Fr	149
Derek Warwick	GB	147
Carlos Reutemann	Arg	146
Emerson Fittipaldi	Bra	144
Jean-Pierre Jarier	Fr	136
Eddie Cheever	US	132
Clay Regazzoni	Swi	132
Martin Brundle	GB	131
Mario Andretti	US	128
Jack Brabham	Aust	126
Ronnie Peterson	Swe	123
Jacky Ickx	Bel	116
Alan Jones	Aust	116
Keke Rosberg	Fin	114
Patrick Tambay	Fr	114
Denny Hulme	NZ	112
Jody Scheckter	SA	112
John Surtees	GB	111
Pierluigi Martini	It	110
Philippe Alliot	Fr	109
Elio de Angelis	It	108
Jochen Mass	Ger	105
Joakim Bonnier	Swe	104
Bruce McLaren	NZ	103

GRAND PRIX WINS PER COUNTRY

Great Britain: 157

Nigel Mansell (31), Jackie Stewart (27), Jim Clark (25), Stirling Moss (16), Graham Hill (14), James Hunt (10), Damon Hill (9), Tony Brooks (6), John Surtees (6), John Watson (5), Peter Collins (3), Mike Hawthorn (3), Peter Gethin (1), Innes Ireland (1)

Ayrton Senna

Brazil: 79

Ayrton Senna (41), Nelson Piquet (23), Emerson Fittipaldi (14), Carlos Pace (1)

France: 77

Alain Prost (51), Rene Arnoux (7), Jacques Laffite (6), Didier Pironi (3), Patrick Depailler (2), Jean-Pierre Jabouille (2), Patrick Tambay (2), Maurice Trintignant (2), Jean-Pierre Beltoise (1), Francois Cevert (1)

Austria: 40

Niki Lauda (25), Gerhard Berger (9), Jochen Rindt (6)

Italy: 39

Alberto Ascari (13), Riccardo Patrese (6), Michele Alboreto (5), Giuseppe Farina (5), Elio de Angelis (2), Giancarlo

Baghetti (1), Lorenzo Bandini (1), Vittorio Brambilla (1), Luigi Fagioli (1), Luigi Musso (1), Alessandro Nannini (1), Ludovico Scarfiotti (1), Piero Taruffi (1)

Argentina: 38

Juan Manual Fangio (24), Carlos Reutemann (12), Jose Froilan Gonzalez (2)

Australia: 26

Jack Brabham (14), Alan Jones (12)

United States: 22

Mario Andretti (12), Dan Gurney (4), Phil Hill (3), Peter Revson (2), Richie Ginther (1)

Germany: 13

Michael Schumacher (10), Wolfgang von Trips (2), Jochen Mass (1)

New Zealand: 12

Denny Hulme (8), Bruce McLaren (4)

Sweden: 12

Ronnie Peterson (10), Jo Bonnier (1), Gunnar Nilsson (1)

Belgium: 11

Jacky Ickx (8), Thierry Boutsen (3)

South Africa: 10

Jody Scheckter (10)

Switzerland: 7

Clay Regazzoni (5), Jo Siffert (2)

Canada: 6

Gilles Villeneuve (6)

Finland: 5

Keke Rosberg (5)

Mexico: 2

Pedro Rodriguez (2)

DRIVERS' WORLD CHAMPION- SHIP WINS PER COUNTRY

Great Britain: 11

Mike Hawthorn (1) 1958 Graham Hill (2) 1962, 1968 Jim Clark (2) 1963, 1965 John Surtees (1) 1964 Jackie Stewart (3) 1969, 1971, 1973 James Hunt (1) 1976 Nigel Mansell (1) 1992

Brazil: 8

Emerson Fittipaldi (2) 1972, 1974 Nelson Piquet (3) 1981, 1983, 1987 Ayrton Senna (3) 1988, 1990, 1991

Argentina: 5

Juan Manuel Fangio (5) 1951, 1954, 1955, 1956, 1957

Australia: 4

Jack Brabham (3) 1959, 1960, 1966 Alan Jones (1) 1980

Austria: 4

Jochen Rindt (1) 1970 Niki Lauda (3) 1975, 1977, 1984

France: 4

Alain Prost (4) 1985, 1986, 1989, 1993

Italy: 3

Nino Farina (1) 1950 Alberto Ascari (2) 1952, 1953

United States: 2

Phil Hill (1) 1961 Mario Andretti (1) 1978

Germany: 1

Michael Schumacher (1) 1994

New Zealand: 1

Denny Hulme (1) 1967

South Africa: 1

Jody Scheckter (1) 1979

Finland: 1

Keke Rosberg (1) 1982

CONSTRUCTORS' GRAND PRIX VICTORIES 1950-1994

Ferrari	104
McLaren	104
Lotus	79
Williams	78
Brabham	35
Tyrrell	23
BRM	17
Cooper	16
Renault	15
Alfa Romeo	10
Maserati	9
Matra	9
Mercedes	9
Vanwall	9
Ligier	8
Benetton	15
March	3
Wolf	3
Honda	2
Eagle	1
Hesketh	1
Penske	1
Porsche	1
Shadow	1

Nigel Mansell: Williams

CONSTRUCTORS'
CHAMPIONSHIP 1958-1994

Year	Constructor	Points	
1958	Vanwall	48	(57)
1959	Cooper-Climax	40	(53)
1960	Cooper-Climax	48	(58)
1961	Ferrari	40	(52)
1962	BRM	42	(56)
1963	Lotus-Climax	54	(74)
1964	Ferrari	45	(49)
1965	Lotus-Climax	54	(58)
1966	Brabham-Repco	42	(49)
1967	Brabham-Repco	63	(67)
1968	Lotus-Ford	62	
1969	Matra-Ford	66	
1970	Lotus-Ford	59	
1971	Tyrrell-Ford	73	
1972	Lotus-Ford	61	
1973	Lotus-Ford	92	(96)
1974	McLaren-Ford	73	(75)
1975	Ferrari	72.5	
1976	Ferrari	83	
1977	Ferrari	95	(97)
1978	Lotus-Ford	86	
1979	Ferrari	113	
1980	Williams-Ford	120	
1981	Williams-Ford	95	
1982	Ferrari	74	
1983	Ferrari	89	
1984	McLaren-TAG	143.5	
1985	McLaren-TAG	90	
1986	Williams-Honda	141	
1987	Williams-Honda	137	
1988	McLaren-Honda	199	
1989	McLaren-Honda	141	
1990	McLaren-Honda	121	
1991	McLaren-Honda	139	
1992	Williams-Renault	164	
1993	Williams-Renault	168	
1994	Williams-Renault	118	

ARGENTINE GRAND PRIX

Races: 16   **First race:** 18/01/1953 - Buenos Aires
Winner: Alberto Ascari
Most wins (driver): Juan Manuel Fangio (4), Emerson Fittipaldi (2)
Most wins (constructor): Ferrari (2), Maserati (2), Cooper (2), Lotus (2), McLaren (2)
Results 1953-81

18/01/53	Buenos Aires	A. Ascari	Ferrari
17/01/54	Buenos Aires	J.M. Fangio	Maserati
16/01/55	Buenos Aires	J.M. Fangio	Mercedes
22/01/56	Buenos Aires	L. Musso/	Lancia-Ferrari
		J.M. Fangio	
13/01/57	Buenos Aires	J.M. Fangio	Maserati
19/01/58	Buenos Aires	S. Moss	Cooper-Climax
07/02/60	Buenos Aires	B. McLaren	Cooper-Climax
23/01/72	Buenos Aires	J. Stewart	Tyrrell-Ford
28/01/73	Buenos Aires	E. Fittipaldi	Lotus-Ford
13/01/74	Buenos Aires	D. Hulme	McLaren-Ford
12/01/75	Buenos Aires	E. Fittipaldi	McLaren-Ford
09/01/77	Buenos Aires	J. Scheckter	Wolf-Ford
15/01/78	Buenos Aires	M. Andretti	Lotus-Ford
21/01/79	Buenos Aires	J. Laffite	Ligier-Ford
13/01/80	Buenos Aires	A. Jones	Williams-Ford
12/04/81	Buenos Aires	N. Piquet	Brabham-Ford

Start of the 1994 Australian Grand Prix

AUSTRALIAN GRAND PRIX

Races: 10   **First race:** 03/11/1985 - Adelaide
Winner: Keke Rosberg
Most wins (driver): Alain Prost (2), Gerhard Berger (2), Ayrton Senna (2)
Most wins (constructor): McLaren (5), Williams (3)

Results 1985-94

03/11/85	Adelaide	K. Rosberg	Williams-Honda
26/10/86	Adelaide	A. Prost	McLaren-TAG
15/11/87	Adelaide	G. Berger	Ferrari
13/11/88	Adelaide	A. Prost	McLaren-Honda
05/11/89	Adelaide	T. Boutsen	Williams-Renault
04/11/90	Adelaide	N. Piquet	Benetton-Ford
03/11/91	Adelaide	A. Senna	McLaren-Honda
08/11/92	Adelaide	G. Berger	McLaren-Honda
07/11/93	Adelaide	A. Senna	McLaren-Ford
13/11/94	Adelaide	N. Mansell	Williams-Renault

AUSTRIAN GRAND PRIX

Races: 19   **First race:** 23/08/1964 - Zeltweg
Winner: Lorenzo Bandini
Most wins (driver): Alain Prost (3), Ronnie Peterson (2), Alan Jones (2)
Most wins (constructor): Lotus (4), McLaren (3)

Results 1964-87

23/08/64	Zeltweg	L. Bandini	Ferrari
16/08/70	Osterreichring	J. Ickx	Ferrari
15/08/71	Osterreichring	J. Siffert	BRM
13/08/72	Osterreichring	E. Fittipaldi	Lotus-Ford
19/08/73	Osterreichring	R. Peterson	Lotus-Ford
18/08/74	Osterreichring	C. Reutemann	Brabham-Ford
17/08/75	Osterreichring	V. Brambilla	March-Ford
15/08/76	Osterreichring	J. Watson	Penske-Ford
14/08/77	Osterreichring	A. Jones	Shadow-Ford
13/08/78	Osterreichring	R. Peterson	Lotus-Ford
12/08/79	Osterreichring	A. Jones	Williams-Ford
17/08/80	Osterreichring	J.P. Jabouille	Renault
16/08/81	Osterreichring	J. Laffite	Ligier-Matra
15/08/82	Osterreichring	E. de Angelis	Lotus-Ford
14/08/83	Osterreichring	A. Prost	Renault
19/08/84	Osterreichring	N. Lauda	McLaren-TAG
18/08/85	Osterreichring	A. Prost	McLaren-TAG
17/08/86	Osterreichring	A. Prost	McLaren-TAG
16/08/87	Osterreichring	N. Mansell	Williams-Honda

BELGIAN GRAND PRIX

Races: 41   **First race:** 18/06/1950 - Spa Francorchamps
Winner: Juan Manuel Fangio
Most wins (driver): Ayrton Senna (5), Jim Clark (4), Juan Manuel Fangio (3)
Most wins (constructor): Ferrari (9), Lotus (8), McLaren (8)

Results 1950-94

18/06/50	Spa	J.M. Fangio	Alfa Romeo
17/06/51	Spa	G. Farina	Alfa Romeo
22/06/52	Spa	A. Ascari	Ferrari
21/06/53	Spa	A. Ascari	Ferrari
20/06/54	Spa	J.M. Fangio	Maserati
05/06/55	Spa	J.M. Fangio	Mercedes
03/06/56	Spa	P. Collins	Lancia-Ferrari
15/06/58	Spa	T. Brooks	Vanwall

19/06/60	Spa	J. Brabham	Cooper-Climax
18/06/61	Spa	P. Hill	Ferrari
17/06/62	Spa	J. Clark	Lotus-Climax
09/06/63	Spa	J. Clark	Lotus-Climax
14/06/64	Spa	J. Clark	Lotus-Climax
13/06/65	Spa	J. Clark	Lotus-Climax
12/06/66	Spa	J. Surtees	Ferrari
18/06/67	Spa	D. Gurney	Eagle-Weslake
09/06/68	Spa	B. McLaren	McLaren-Ford
07/06/70	Spa	P. Rodriguez	BRM
04/06/72	Nivelles	E. Fittipaldi	Lotus-Ford
20/05/73	Zolder	J. Stewart	Tyrrell-Ford
12/05/74	Nivelles	E. Fittipaldi	McLaren-Ford
25/05/75	Zolder	N. Lauda	Ferrari
16/05/76	Zolder	N. Lauda	Ferrari
05/06/77	Zolder	G. Nilsson	Lotus-Ford
21/05/78	Zolder	M. Andretti	Lotus-Ford
13/05/79	Zolder	J. Scheckter	Ferrari
04/05/80	Zolder	D. Pironi	Ligier-Ford
17/05/81	Zolder	C. Reutemann	Williams-Ford
09/05/82	Zolder	J. Watson	McLaren-Ford
22/05/83	Spa	A. Prost	Renault
29/04/84	Zolder	M. Alboreto	Ferrari
15/09/85	Spa	A. Senna	Lotus-Renault
25/05/86	Spa	N. Mansell	Williams-Honda
17/05/87	Spa	A. Prost	McLaren-TAG
28/08/88	Spa	A. Senna	McLaren-Honda
27/08/89	Spa	A. Senna	McLaren-Honda
26/08/90	Spa	A. Senna	McLaren-Honda
25/08/91	Spa	A. Senna	McLaren-Honda
30/08/92	Spa	M. Schumacher	Benetton-Ford
29/08/93	Spa	D. Hill	Williams-Renault
28/08/94	Spa	D. Hill	Williams-Renault

BRAZILIAN GRAND PRIX

Races: 22   **First race:** 11/02/1973 - Interlagos
Winner: Emerson Fittipaldi
Most wins (driver): Alain Prost (6), Carlos Reutemann (3)
Most wins (constructor): McLaren (7), Ferrari (5)
Results 1973-94

11/02/73	Interlagos	E. Fittipaldi	Lotus-Ford
27/01/74	Interlagos	E. Fittipaldi	McLaren-Ford
26/01/75	Interlagos	C. Pace	Brabham-Ford
25/01/76	Interlagos	N. Lauda	Ferrari
23/01/77	Interlagos	C. Reutemann	Ferrari
29/01/78	Rio de Janeiro	C. Reutemann	Ferrari
04/02/79	Interlagos	J. Laffite	Ligier-Ford
27/01/80	Interlagos	R. Arnoux	Renault
29/03/81	Rio de Janeiro	C. Reutemann	Williams-Ford
21/03/82	Rio de Janeiro	A. Prost	Renault
13/03/83	Rio de Janeiro	N. Piquet	Brabham-BMW
25/03/84	Rio de Janeiro	A. Prost	McLaren-TAG
07/04/85	Rio de Janeiro	A. Prost	McLaren-TAG
23/03/86	Rio de Janeiro	N. Piquet	Williams-Honda
12/04/87	Rio de Janeiro	A. Prost	McLaren-TAG

03/04/88	Rio de Janeiro	A. Prost	McLaren-Honda
26/03/89	Rio de Janeiro	N. Mansell	Ferrari
25/03/90	Interlagos	A. Prost	Ferrari
24/03/91	Interlagos	A. Senna	McLaren-Honda
05/04/92	Interlagos	N. Mansell	Williams-Renault
28/03/93	Interlagos	A. Senna	McLaren-Ford
27/03/94	Interlagos	M. Schumacher	Benetton-Ford

BRITISH GRAND PRIX

Races: 45 **First race:** 13/05/1950 - Silverstone
Winner: Giuseppe Farina
Most wins (driver): Jim Clark (5), Alain Prost (5), Nigel Mansell (4)
Most wins (constructor): Ferrari (10), McLaren (9), Lotus (8), Williams (8)
Results 1950-1994

13/05/50	Silverstone	G. Farina	Alfa Romeo
14/07/51	Silverstone	J.F. Gonzalez	Ferrari
19/07/52	Silverstone	A. Ascari	Ferrari
18/07/53	Silverstone	A. Ascari	Ferrari
17/07/54	Silverstone	J.F. Gonzalez	Ferrari
16/07/55	Aintree	S. Moss	Mercedes
14/07/56	Silverstone	J.M. Fangio	Lancia-Ferrari
20/07/57	Aintree	T. Brooks/S. Moss	Vanwall
19/07/58	Silverstone	P. Collins	Ferrari
18/07/59	Aintree	J. Brabham	Cooper-Climax
16/07/60	Silverstone	J. Brabham	Cooper-Climax
15/07/61	Aintree	W. von Trips	Ferrari
21/07/62	Aintree	J. Clark	Lotus-Climax
20/07/63	Silverstone	J. Clark	Lotus-Climax
11/07/64	Brands Hatch	J. Clark	Lotus-Climax
10/07/65	Silverstone	J. Clark	Lotus-Climax
16/07/66	Brands Hatch	J. Brabham	Brabham-Repco
15/07/67	Silverstone	J. Clark	Lotus-Ford
20/07/68	Brands Hatch	J. Siffert	Lotus-Ford
19/07/69	Silverstone	J. Stewart	Matra-Ford
18/07/70	Brands Hatch	J. Rindt	Lotus-Ford
17/07/71	Silverstone	J. Stewart	Tyrrell-Ford
15/07/72	Brands Hatch	E. Fittipaldi	Lotus-Ford
14/07/73	Silverstone	P. Revson	McLaren-Ford
20/07/74	Brands Hatch	J. Scheckter	Tyrrell-Ford
19/07/75	Silverstone	E. Fittipaldi	McLaren-Ford
18/07/76	Brands Hatch	N. Lauda	Ferrari
16/07/77	Silverstone	J. Hunt	McLaren-Ford
16/07/78	Brands Hatch	C. Reutemann	Ferrari
14/07/79	Silverstone	C. Regazzoni	Williams-Ford
13/07/80	Brands Hatch	A. Jones	Williams-Ford
18/07/81	Silverstone	J. Watson	McLaren-Ford
18/07/82	Brands Hatch	N. Lauda	McLaren-Ford
16/07/83	Silverstone	A. Prost	Renault
22/07/84	Brands Hatch	N. Lauda	McLaren-TAG
21/07/85	Silverstone	A. Prost	McLaren-TAG
13/07/86	Brands Hatch	N. Mansell	Williams-Honda
12/07/87	Silverstone	N. Mansell	Williams-Honda
10/07/88	Silverstone	A. Senna	McLaren-Honda

16/07/89	Silverstone	A. Prost	McLaren-Honda
15/07/90	Silverstone	A. Prost	Ferrari
14/07/91	Silverstone	N. Mansell	Williams-Renault
12/07/92	Silverstone	N. Mansell	Williams-Renault
11/07/93	Silverstone	A. Prost	Williams-Renault
10/07/94	Silverstone	D. Hill	Williams-Renault

1994 Canadian Grand Prix

CANADIAN GRAND PRIX

Races: 26   **First race:** 27/08/1967 - Mosport Park
Winner: Jack Brabham
Most wins (driver): Nelson Piquet (3)
Most wins (constructor): McLaren (7), Williams (5)
Results 1967-94

27/08/67	Mosport Park	J. Brabham	Brabham-Repco
22/09/68	St Jovite	D. Hulme	McLaren-Ford
20/09/69	Mosport Park	J. Ickx	Brabham-Ford
20/09/70	St Jovite	J. Ickx	Ferrari
19/09/71	Mosport Park	J. Stewart	Tyrrell-Ford
24/09/72	Mosport Park	J. Stewart	Tyrrell-Ford
23/09/73	Mosport Park	P. Revson	McLaren-Ford
22/09/74	Mosport Park	E. Fittipaldi	McLaren-Ford
03/10/76	Mosport Park	J. Hunt	McLaren-Ford
09/10/77	Mosport Park	J. Scheckter	Wolf-Ford
08/10/78	Montreal	G. Villeneuve	Ferrari
30/09/79	Montreal	A. Jones	Williams-Ford
28/09/80	Montreal	A. Jones	Williams-Ford
27/09/81	Montreal	J. Laffite	Ligier-Matra
13/06/82	Montreal	N. Piquet	Brabham-BMW
12/06/83	Montreal	R. Arnoux	Ferrari
17/06/84	Montreal	N. Piquet	Brabham-BMW
16/06/85	Montreal	M. Alboreto	Ferrari
15/06/86	Montreal	N. Mansell	Williams-Honda
12/06/88	Montreal	A. Senna	McLaren-Honda

18/06/89	Montreal	T. Boutsen	Williams-Renault
10/06/90	Montreal	A. Senna	McLaren-Honda
02/06/91	Montreal	N. Piquet	Benetton-Ford
14/06/92	Montreal	G. Berger	McLaren-Honda
13/06/93	Montreal	A. Prost	Williams-Renault
21/06/94	Montreal	M. Schumacher	Benetton-Ford

DALLAS GRAND PRIX

Races: 1   **First race:** 08/07/1984 – Fir Park
Winner: Keke Rosberg
Most wins (driver): Keke Rosberg (1)
Most wins (constructor): Williams (1)
Result 1984

08/07/84	Fir Park	K. Rosberg	Williams-Honda

DETROIT GRAND PRIX

Races: 5   **First race:** 06/06/1982 – Detroit
Winner: John Watson
Most wins (driver): John Watson (1), Michele Alboreto (1), Nelson Piquet (1), Keke Rosberg (1), Ayrton Senna (1)
Most wins (constructor): McLaren (1), Tyrrell (1), Brabham (1), Williams (1), Lotus (1)
Results 1982-86

06/06/82	Detroit	J. Watson	McLaren-Ford
05/06/83	Detroit	M. Alboreto	Tyrrell-Ford
24/06/84	Detroit	N. Piquet	Brabham-BMW
23/06/85	Detroit	K. Rosberg	Williams-Honda
22/06/86	Detroit	A. Senna	Lotus-Renault

DUTCH GRAND PRIX

Races: 30   **First race:** 17/08/1952 – Zandvoort
Winner: Alberto Ascari
Most wins (driver): Jim Clark (4), Niki Lauda (3), Jackie Stewart (3)
Most wins (constructor): Ferrari (8), Lotus (6)
Results 1952-85

17/08/52	Zandvoort	A. Ascari	Ferrari
07/06/53	Zandvoort	A. Ascari	Ferrari
19/06/55	Zandvoort	J.M. Fangio	Mercedes
26/05/58	Zandvoort	S. Moss	Vanwall
31/05/59	Zandvoort	J. Bonnier	BRM
06/06/60	Zandvoort	J. Brabham	Cooper-Climax
22/05/61	Zandvoort	W. von Trips	Ferrari
20/05/62	Zandvoort	G. Hill	BRM
23/06/63	Zandvoort	J. Clark	Lotus-Climax
24/05/64	Zandvoort	J. Clark	Lotus-Climax
18/07/65	Zandvoort	J. Clark	Lotus-Climax
24/07/66	Zandvoort	J. Brabham	Brabham-Repco
04/06/67	Zandvoort	J. Clark	Lotus-Ford
23/06/68	Zandvoort	J. Stewart	Matra-Ford
21/06/69	Zandvoort	J. Stewart	Matra-Ford
21/06/70	Zandvoort	J. Rindt	Lotus-Ford
20/06/71	Zandvoort	J. Ickx	Ferrari

29/07/73	Zandvoort	J. Stewart	Tyrrell-Ford
23/06/74	Zandvoort	N. Lauda	Ferrari
22/06/75	Zandvoort	J. Hunt	Hesketh-Ford
29/08/76	Zandvoort	J. Hunt	McLaren-Ford
28/08/77	Zandvoort	N. Lauda	Ferrari
27/08/78	Zandvoort	M. Andretti	Lotus-Ford
26/08/79	Zandvoort	A. Jones	Williams-Ford
31/08/80	Zandvoort	N. Piquet	Brabham-Ford
30/08/81	Zandvoort	A. Prost	Renault
03/07/82	Zandvoort	D. Pironi	Ferrari
28/08/83	Zandvoort	R. Arnoux	Ferrari
26/08/84	Zandvoort	A. Prost	McLaren-TAG
25/08/85	Zandvoort	N. Lauda	McLaren-TAG

Frentzen, Herbert, Panis and Alesi in the 1994 European Grand Prix

EUROPEAN GRAND PRIX

Races: 5   **First race:** 25/09/1983 - Brands Hatch
Winner: Nelson Piquet
Most wins (driver): Nelson Piquet (1), Alain Prost (1), Nigel Mansell (1), Ayrton Senna (1), Michael Schumacher (1)
Most wins (constructor): McLaren (2)
Results 1983-94

25/09/83	Brands Hatch	N. Piquet	Brabham-BMW
07/10/84	Nurburgring	A. Prost	McLaren-Tag
06/10/85	Brands Hatch	N. Mansell	Williams-Honda
11/04/93	Donington	A. Senna	McLaren-Ford
16/10/94	Jerez	M. Schumacher	Benetton-Ford

FRENCH GRAND PRIX

Races: 44   **First race:** 02/07/1950 - Reims
Winner: Juan Manuel Fangio
Most wins (driver): Alain Prost (6), Juan Manuel Fangio (4), Nigel Mansell (4)
Most wins (constructor): Ferrari (9), Lotus (7)

Results 1950-94

02/07/50	Reims	J.M. Fangio	Alfa Romeo
01/07/51	Reims	L. Fagioli/	Alfa Romeo
		J.M. Fangio	
06/07/52	Rouen	A. Ascari	Ferrari
05/07/53	Reims	M. Hawthorn	Ferrari
04/07/54	Reims	J.M. Fangio	Mercedes
01/07/56	Reims	P. Collins	Lancia-Ferrari
07/07/57	Rouen	J.M. Fangio	Maserati
06/07/58	Reims	M. Hawthorn	Ferrari
05/07/59	Reims	T. Brooks	Ferrari
03/07/60	Reims	J. Brabham	Cooper-Climax
02/07/61	Reims	G. Baghetti	Ferrari
08/07/62	Rouen	D. Gurney	Porsche
30/06/63	Reims	J. Clark	Lotus-Climax
28/06/64	Rouen	D. Gurney	Brabham-Climax
27/06/65	Clermont-Ferrand	J. Clark	Lotus-Climax
03/07/66	Reims	J. Brabham	Brabham-Repco
02/07/67	Le Mans	J. Brabham	Brabham-Repco
07/07/68	Rouen	J. Ickx	Ferrari
06/07/69	Clermont-Ferrand	J. Stewart	Matra-Ford
05/07/70	Clermont-Ferrand	J. Rindt	Lotus-Ford
04/07/71	Paul Ricard	J. Stewart	Tyrrell-Ford
02/07/72	Clermont-Ferrand	J. Stewart	Tyrrell-Ford
01/07/73	Paul Ricard	R. Peterson	Lotus-Ford
07/07/74	Dijon	R. Peterson	Lotus-Ford
06/07/75	Paul Ricard	N. Lauda	Ferrari
04/07/76	Paul Ricard	J. Hunt	McLaren-Ford
03/07/77	Dijon	M. Andretti	Lotus-Ford
02/07/78	Paul Ricard	M. Andretti	Lotus-Ford
01/07/79	Dijon	J.P. Jabouille	Renault
29/06/80	Paul Ricard	A. Jones	Williams-Ford
05/07/81	Dijon	A. Prost	Renault
25/07/82	Paul Ricard	R. Arnoux	Renault
17/04/83	Paul Ricard	A. Prost	Renault
20/05/84	Dijon	N. Lauda	McLaren-TAG
07/07/85	Paul Ricard	N. Piquet	Brabham-BMW
06/07/86	Paul Ricard	N. Mansell	Williams-Honda
05/07/87	Paul Ricard	N. Mansell	Williams-Honda
03/07/88	Paul Ricard	A. Prost	McLaren-Honda
09/07/89	Paul Ricard	A. Prost	McLaren-Honda
08/07/90	Paul Ricard	A. Prost	Ferrari
07/07/91	Magny-Cours	N. Mansell	Williams-Renault
05/07/92	Magny-Cours	N. Mansell	Williams-Renault
04/07/93	Magny-Cours	A. Prost	Williams-Renault
03/07/94	Magny-Cours	M. Schumacher	Benetton-Ford

GERMAN GRAND PRIX

Races: 42 **First race:** 29/07/1951 - Nurburgring
Winner: Alberto Ascari
Most wins (driver): Juan Manuel Fangio (3), Jackie Stewart (3), Nelson Piquet (3), Ayrton Senna (3)
Most wins (constructor): Ferrari (14)
Results 1951-1994

29/07/51	Nurburgring	A. Ascari	Ferrari

03/08/52	Nurburgring	A. Ascari	Ferrari
02/08/53	Nurburgring	G. Farina	Ferrari
01/08/54	Nurburgring	J.M. Fangio	Mercedes
05/08/56	Nurburgring	J.M. Fangio	Lancia-Ferrari
04/08/57	Nurburgring	J.M. Fangio	Maserati
03/08/58	Nurburgring	T. Brooks	Vanwall
02/08/59	Avus	T. Brooks	Ferrari
06/08/61	Nurburgring	S. Moss	Lotus-Climax
05/08/62	Nurburgring	G. Hill	BRM
04/08/63	Nurburgring	J. Surtees	Ferrari
02/08/64	Nurburgring	J. Surtees	Ferrari
01/08/65	Nurburgring	J. Clark	Lotus-Climax
07/08/66	Nurburgring	J. Brabham	Brabham-Repco
06/08/67	Nurburgring	D. Hulme	Brabham-Repco
04/08/68	Nurburgring	J. Stewart	Matra-Ford
03/08/69	Nurburgring	J. Ickx	Brabham-Ford
02/08/70	Hockenheim	J. Rindt	Lotus-Ford
01/08/71	Nurburgring	J. Stewart	Tyrrell-Ford
30/07/72	Nurburgring	J. Ickx	Ferrari
05/08/73	Nurburgring	J. Stewart	Tyrrell-Ford
04/08/74	Nurburgring	C. Regazzoni	Ferrari
03/08/75	Nurburgring	C. Reutemann	Brabham-Ford
01/08/76	Nurburgring	J. Hunt	McLaren-Ford
31/07/77	Hockenheim	N. Lauda	Ferrari
30/07/78	Hockenheim	M. Andretti	Lotus-Ford
29/07/79	Hockenheim	A. Jones	Williams-Ford
10/08/80	Hockenheim	J. Laffite	Ligier-Ford
02/08/81	Hockenheim	N. Piquet	Brabham-Ford
08/08/82	Hockenheim	P. Tambay	Ferrari
07/08/83	Hockenheim	R. Arnoux	Ferrari
05/08/84	Hockenheim	A. Prost	McLaren-TAG
04/08/85	Nurburgring	M. Alboreto	Ferrari
27/07/86	Hockenheim	N. Piquet	Williams-Honda
26/07/87	Hockenheim	N. Piquet	Williams-Honda
24/07/88	Hockenheim	A. Senna	McLaren-Honda
30/07/89	Hockenheim	A. Senna	McLaren-Honda
29/07/90	Hockenheim	A. Senna	McLaren-Honda
28/07/91	Hockenheim	N. Mansell	Williams-Renault
26/07/92	Hockenheim	N. Mansell	Williams-Renault
25/07/93	Hockenheim	A. Prost	Williams-Renault
31/07/94	Hockenheim	G. Berger	Ferrari

HUNGARIAN GRAND PRIX

Races: 9　　　　**First race:** 10/08/1986 - Hungaroring
Winner: Nelson Piquet
Most wins (driver): Ayrton Senna (3), Nelson Piquet (2)
Most wins (constructor): Williams (4), McLaren (3)
Results 1986-94

10/08/86	Hungaroring	N. Piquet	Williams-Honda
09/08/87	Hungaroring	N. Piquet	Williams-Honda
07/08/88	Hungaroring	A. Senna	McLaren-Honda
13/08/89	Hungaroring	N. Mansell	Ferrari
12/08/90	Hungaroring	T. Boutsen	Williams-Renault
11/08/91	Hungaroring	A. Senna	McLaren-Honda
16/08/92	Hungaroring	A. Senna	McLaren-Honda

| 15/08/93 | Hungaroring | D. Hill | Williams-Renault |
| 14/08/94 | Hungaroring | M. Schumacher | Benetton-Ford |

ITALIAN GRAND PRIX

Races: 45   **First race:** 03/09/50 - Monza
Winner: Giuseppe Farina
Most wins (driver): Nelson Piquet (4), Juan Manuel Fangio (3),
Stirling Moss (3), Ronnie Peterson (3), Alain Prost (3)
Most wins (constructor): Ferrari (10)
Results 1950-1994

03/09/50	Monza	G. Farina	Alfa Romeo
16/09/51	Monza	A. Ascari	Ferrari
07/09/52	Monza	A. Ascari	Ferrari
13/09/53	Monza	J.M. Fangio	Maserati
05/09/54	Monza	J.M. Fangio	Mercedes
11/09/55	Monza	J.M. Fangio	Mercedes
02/09/56	Monza	S. Moss	Maserati
08/09/57	Monza	S. Moss	Vanwall
07/09/58	Monza	T. Brooks	Vanwall
13/09/59	Monza	S. Moss	Cooper-Climax
04/09/60	Monza	P. Hill	Ferrari
10/09/61	Monza	P. Hill	Ferrari
16/09/62	Monza	G. Hill	BRM
08/09/63	Monza	J. Clark	Lotus-Climax
06/09/64	Monza	J. Surtees	Ferrari
12/09/65	Monza	J. Stewart	BRM
04/09/66	Monza	L. Scarfiotti	Ferrari
10/09/67	Monza	J. Surtees	Honda
08/09/68	Monza	D. Hulme	McLaren-Ford
07/09/69	Monza	J. Stewart	Matra-Ford
06/09/70	Monza	C. Regazzoni	Ferrari
05/09/71	Monza	P. Gethin	BRM
10/09/72	Monza	E. Fittipaldi	Lotus-Ford
09/09/73	Monza	R. Peterson	Lotus-Ford
08/09/74	Monza	R. Peterson	Lotus-Ford
07/09/75	Monza	C. Regazzoni	Ferrari
12/09/76	Monza	R. Peterson	March-Ford
11/09/77	Monza	M. Andretti	Lotus-Ford
10/09/78	Monza	N. Lauda	Brabham-Alfa
09/09/79	Monza	J. Scheckter	Ferrari
14/09/80	Imola	N. Piquet	Brabham-Ford
13/09/81	Monza	A. Prost	Renault
12/09/82	Monza	R. Arnoux	Renault
11/09/83	Monza	N. Piquet	Brabham-BMW
09/09/84	Monza	N. Lauda	McLaren-TAG
08/09/85	Monza	A. Prost	McLaren-TAG
07/09/86	Monza	N. Piquet	Williams-Honda
06/09/87	Monza	N. Piquet	Williams-Honda
11/09/88	Monza	G. Berger	Ferrari
10/09/89	Monza	A. Prost	McLaren-Honda
09/09/90	Monza	A. Senna	McLaren-Honda
08/09/91	Monza	N. Mansell	Williams-Renault
13/09/92	Monza	A. Senna	McLaren-Honda
12/09/93	Monza	D. Hill	Williams-Renault
11/09/94	Monza	D. Hill	Williams-Renault

JAPANESE GRAND PRIX

Races: 10   **First race:** 24/10/1976 - Fuji
Winner: Mario Andretti
Most wins (driver): Ayrton Senna (2), Gerhard Berger (2)
Most wins (constructor): McLaren (5)
Results 1976-94

24/10/76	Fuji	M. Andretti	Lotus-Ford
23/10/77	Fuji	J. Hunt	McLaren-Ford
01/11/87	Suzuka	G. Berger	Ferrari
30/10/88	Suzuka	A. Senna	McLaren-Honda
22/10/89	Suzuka	A. Nannini	Benetton-Ford
21/10/90	Suzuka	N. Piquet	Benetton-Ford
20/10/91	Suzuka	G. Berger	McLaren-Honda
25/10/92	Suzuka	R. Patrese	Williams-Renault
24/10/93	Suzuka	A. Senna	McLaren-Ford
06/11/94	Suzuka	D. Hill	Williams-Renault

LAS VEGAS GRAND PRIX

Races: 2   **First race:** 17/10/1981 - Caesar's Palace
Winner: Alan Jones
Most wins (driver): Alan Jones (1), Michele Alboreto (1)
Most wins (constructor): Williams (1), Tyrrell (1)
Results 1981-82

17/10/81	Caesar's Palace	A. Jones	Williams-Ford
25/09/82	Caesar's Palace	M. Alboreto	Tyrrell-Ford

MEXICAN GRAND PRIX

Races: 15   **First race:** 27/10/1963 - Mexico City
Winner: Jim Clark
Most wins (driver): Jim Clark (2), Nigel Mansell (2), Alain Prost (2)
Most wins (constructor): Lotus (3), McLaren (3), Williams (3)
Results 1963-1992

27/10/63	Mexico City	J. Clark	Lotus-Climax
25/10/64	Mexico City	D. Gurney	Brabham-Climax
24/10/65	Mexico City	R. Ginther	Honda
23/10/66	Mexico City	J. Surtees	Cooper-Maserati
22/10/67	Mexico City	J. Clark	Lotus-Ford
03/11/68	Mexico City	G. Hill	Lotus-Ford
19/10/69	Mexico City	D. Hulme	McLaren-Ford
25/10/70	Mexico City	J. Ickx	Ferrari
12/10/86	Mexico City	G. Berger	Benetton-BMW
18/10/87	Mexico City	N. Mansell	Williams-Honda
29/05/88	Mexico City	A. Prost	McLaren-Honda
28/05/89	Mexico City	A. Senna	McLaren-Honda
24/06/90	Mexico City	A. Prost	Ferrari
16/06/91	Mexico City	R. Patrese	Williams-Renault
22/03/92	Mexico City	N. Mansell	Williams-Renault

MONACO GRAND PRIX

Races: 41
First race: 21/05/1950 - Monte Carlo

*Schumacher (1st), Brundle (2nd), Berger (3rd): 1994
Monaco Grand Prix*

Winner: Juan Manuel Fangio
Most wins (driver): Ayrton Senna (6), Graham Hill (5), Alain
Prost (4), Stirling Moss (3), Jackie Stewart (3)
Most wins (constructor): McLaren (9), Lotus (7), Ferrari (5),
BRM (5)

Results 1950-94

21/05/50	Monte Carlo	J.M. Fangio	Alfa Romeo
22/05/55	Monte Carlo	M. Trintignant	Ferrari
13/05/56	Monte Carlo	S. Moss	Maserati
19/05/57	Monte Carlo	J.M. Fangio	Maserati
18/05/58	Monte Carlo	M. Trintignant	Cooper-Climax
10/05/59	Monte Carlo	J. Brabham	Cooper-Climax
29/05/60	Monte Carlo	S. Moss	Lotus-Climax
14/05/61	Monte Carlo	S. Moss	Lotus-Climax
03/06/62	Monte Carlo	B. McLaren	Cooper-Climax
26/05/63	Monte Carlo	G. Hill	BRM
10/05/64	Monte Carlo	G. Hill	BRM
30/05/65	Monte Carlo	G. Hill	BRM
22/05/66	Monte Carlo	J. Stewart	BRM
07/05/67	Monte Carlo	D. Hulme	Brabham-Repco
26/05/68	Monte Carlo	G. Hill	Lotus-Ford
18/05/69	Monte Carlo	G. Hill	Lotus-Ford
10/05/70	Monte Carlo	J. Rindt	Lotus-Ford
23/05/71	Monte Carlo	J. Stewart	Tyrrell-Ford
14/05/72	Monte Carlo	J.P. Beltoise	BRM
03/06/73	Monte Carlo	J. Stewart	Tyrrell-Ford
26/05/74	Monte Carlo	R. Peterson	Lotus-Ford
11/05/75	Monte Carlo	N. Lauda	Ferrari
30/05/76	Monte Carlo	N. Lauda	Ferrari
22/05/77	Monte Carlo	J. Scheckter	Wolf-Ford
07/05/78	Monte Carlo	P. Depailler	Tyrrell-Ford
27/05/79	Monte Carlo	J. Scheckter	Ferrari
18/05/80	Monte Carlo	C. Reutemann	Williams-Ford

31/05/81	Monte Carlo	G. Villeneuve	Ferrari
23/05/82	Monte Carlo	R. Patrese	Brabham-Ford
15/05/83	Monte Carlo	K. Rosberg	Williams-Ford
03/06/84	Monte Carlo	A. Prost	McLaren-TAG
19/05/85	Monte Carlo	A. Prost	McLaren-TAG
11/05/86	Monte Carlo	A. Prost	McLaren-TAG
31/05/87	Monte Carlo	A. Senna	Lotus-Honda
15/05/88	Monte Carlo	A. Prost	McLaren-Honda
07/05/89	Monte Carlo	A. Senna	McLaren-Honda
27/05/90	Monte Carlo	A. Senna	McLaren-Honda
12/05/91	Monte Carlo	A. Senna	McLaren-Honda
31/05/92	Monte Carlo	A. Senna	McLaren-Honda
23/05/93	Monte Carlo	A. Senna	McLaren-Ford
15/05/94	Monte Carlo	M. Schumacher	Benetton-Ford

MOROCCAN GRAND PRIX

Races: 1   **First race:** 19/10/1958 - Casablanca
Winner: Stirling Moss
Most wins (driver): Stirling Moss (1)
Most wins (constructor): Vanwall (1)
Result 1958
19/10/58	Casablanca	S. Moss	Vanwall

PESCARA GRAND PRIX

Races: 1   **First race:** 18/08/1957 - Pescara
Winner: Stirling Moss
Most wins (driver): Stirling Moss (1)
Most wins (constructor): Vanwall
Result 1957
18/08/57	Pescara	S. Moss	Vanwall

PACIFIC GRAND PRIX

Races: 1   **First race:** 17/04/1994 - Aida
Winner: Michael Schumacher
Most wins (driver): Michael Schumacher (1)
Most wins (constructor): Benetton (1)
Result 1994
17/04/94	Aida	M. Schumacher	Benetton-Ford

PORTUGUESE GRAND PRIX

Races: 14   **First race:** 14/08/1958 - Oporto
Winner: Stirling Moss
Most wins (driver): Alain Prost (3), Nigel Mansell (3), Stirling Moss (2)
Most wins (constructor): Williams (4), McLaren (3)
Results 1958-94
24/08/58	Oporto	S. Moss	Vanwall
23/08/59	Monsanto	S. Moss	Cooper-Climax
14/08/60	Oporto	J. Brabham	Cooper-Climax
21/10/84	Estoril	A. Prost	McLaren-TAG
21/04/85	Estoril	A. Senna	Lotus-Renault
21/09/86	Estoril	N. Mansell	Williams-Honda
20/09/87	Estoril	A. Prost	McLaren-TAG

25/09/88	Estoril	A. Prost	McLaren-Honda
24/09/89	Estoril	G. Berger	Ferrari
23/09/90	Estoril	N. Mansell	Ferrari
22/09/91	Estoril	R. Patrese	Williams-Renault
27/09/92	Estoril	N. Mansell	Williams-Renault
26/09/93	Estoril	M. Schumacher	Benetton-Ford
25/09/94	Estoril	D. Hill	Williams-Renault

SAN MARINO GRAND PRIX

Races: 14   **First race:** 03/05/1981 - Imola
Winner: Nelson Piquet
Most wins (driver): Alain Prost (3), Ayrton Senna (3), Nigel Mansell (2)
Most wins (constructor): McLaren (5), Williams (4)
Results 1981-94

03/05/81	Imola	N. Piquet	Brabham-Ford
25/04/82	Imola	D. Pironi	Ferrari
01/05/83	Imola	P. Tambay	Ferrari
06/05/84	Imola	A. Prost	McLaren-TAG
05/05/85	Imola	E. de Angelis	Lotus-Renault
27/04/86	Imola	A. Prost	McLaren-TAG
03/05/87	Imola	N. Mansell	Williams-Honda
01/05/88	Imola	A. Senna	McLaren-Honda
23/04/89	Imola	A. Senna	McLaren-Honda
13/05/90	Imola	R. Patrese	Williams-Renault
28/04/91	Imola	A. Senna	McLaren-Honda
17/05/92	Imola	N. Mansell	Williams-Renault
25/04/93	Imola	A. Prost	Williams-Renault
01/05/94	Imola	M. Schumacher	Benetton-Ford

SOUTH AFRICAN GRAND PRIX

Races: 23   **First race:** 29/12/1962 - East London
Winner: Graham Hill
Most wins (driver): Jim Clark (3), Niki Lauda (3), Jackie Stewart (2), Alain Prost (2), Nigel Mansell (2)
Most wins (constructor): Lotus (4), Ferrari (4)
Results 1962-93

29/12/62	East London	G. Hill	BRM
28/12/63	East London	J. Clark	Lotus-Climax
01/01/65	East London	J. Clark	Lotus-Climax
02/01/67	Kyalami	P. Rodriguez	Cooper-Maserati
01/01/68	Kyalami	J. Clark	Lotus-Ford
01/03/69	Kyalami	J. Stewart	Matra-Ford
07/03/70	Kyalami	J. Brabham	Brabham-Ford
06/03/71	Kyalami	M. Andretti	Ferrari
04/03/72	Kyalami	D. Hulme	McLaren-Ford
03/03/73	Kyalami	J. Stewart	Tyrrell-Ford
30/03/74	Kyalami	C. Reutemann	Brabham-Ford
01/03/75	Kyalami	J. Scheckter	Tyrrell-Ford
06/03/76	Kyalami	N. Lauda	Ferrari
05/03/77	Kyalami	N. Lauda	Ferrari
04/03/78	Kyalami	R. Peterson	Lotus-Ford
03/03/79	Kyalami	G. Villeneuve	Ferrari
01/03/80	Kyalami	R. Arnoux	Renault

23/01/82	Kyalami	A. Prost	Renault
16/10/83	Kyalami	R. Patrese	Brabham-BMW
07/04/84	Kyalami	N. Lauda	McLaren-TAG
19/10/85	Kyalami	N. Mansell	Williams-Honda
01/03/92	Kyalami	N. Mansell	Williams-Renault
14/03/93	Kyalami	A. Prost	Wiiliams-Renault

SPANISH GRAND PRIX

Races: 24   **First race:** 28/10/1951 - Pedralbes
Winner: Juan Manuel Fangio
Most wins (driver): Jackie Stewart (3), Nigel Mansell (3), Alain Prost (3)
Most wins (constructor): Lotus (6), Williams (5)
Results 1951-94

28/10/51	Pedralbes	J.M. Fangio	Alfa Romeo
24/10/54	Pedralbes	M. Hawthorn	Ferrari
12/05/68	Jarama	G. Hill	Lotus-Ford
04/05/69	Montjuich Park	J. Stewart	Matra-Ford
19/04/70	Jarama	J. Stewart	March-Ford
18/04/71	Montjuich Park	J. Stewart	Tyrrell-Ford
01/05/72	Jarama	E. Fittipaldi	Lotus-Ford
29/04/73	Montjuich Park	E. Fittipaldi	Lotus-Ford
28/04/74	Jarama	N. Lauda	Ferrari
27/04/75	Montjuich Park	J. Mass	McLaren-Ford
02/05/76	Jarama	J. Hunt	McLaren-Ford
08/05/77	Jarama	M. Andretti	Lotus-Ford
04/06/78	Jarama	M. Andretti	Lotus-Ford
29/04/79	Jarama	P. Depailler	Ligier-Ford
21/06/81	Jarama	G. Villeneuve	Ferrari
13/04/86	Jerez	A. Senna	Lotus-Renault
27/09/87	Jerez	N. Mansell	Williams-Honda
02/10/88	Jerez	A. Prost	McLaren-Honda
01/10/89	Jerez	A. Senna	McLaren-Honda
30/09/90	Jerez	A. Prost	Ferrari
29/09/91	Barcelona	N. Mansell	Williams-Renault
03/05/92	Barcelona	N. Mansell	Williams-Renault
09/05/93	Barcelona	A. Prost	Williams-Renault
29/05/94	Barcelona	D. Hill	Williams-Renault

SWEDISH GRAND PRIX

Races: 6   **First race:** 17/06/1973 - Anderstorp
Winners: Denny Hulme
Most wins (driver): Jody Scheckter (2), Niki Lauda (2)
Most wins (constructor): Tyrrell (2)
Results 1973-78

17/06/73	Anderstorp	D. Hulme	McLaren-Ford
09/06/74	Anderstorp	J. Scheckter	Tyrrell-Ford
08/06/75	Anderstorp	N. Lauda	Ferrari
13/06/76	Anderstorp	J. Scheckter	Tyrrell-Ford
19/06/77	Anderstorp	J. Laffite	Ligier-Matra
17/06/78	Anderstorp	N. Lauda	Brabham-Alfa

SWISS GRAND PRIX

Races: 6   **First race:** 04/06/1950 - Bremgarten
Winner: Giuseppe Farina
Most wins (driver): Juan Manuel Fangio (2)
Most wins (constructor): Alfa Romeo (2), Ferrari (2)
Results 1950-82

04/06/50	Bremgarten	G. Farina	Alfa Romeo
27/05/51	Bremgarten	J.M. Fangio	Alfa Romeo
18/05/52	Bremgarten	P. Taruffi	Ferrari
23/08/53	Bremgarten	A. Ascari	Ferrari
22/08/54	Bremgarten	J.M. Fangio	Mercedes
29/08/82	Dijon	K. Rosberg	Williams-Ford

UNITED STATES GRAND PRIX

Races: 22   **First race:** 12/12/1959 - Sebring
Winner: Bruce McLaren
Most wins (driver): Ayrton Senna (4), Graham Hill (3), Jim Clark (3)
Most wins (constructor): Lotus (9)
Results 1959-91

12/12/59	Sebring	B. McLaren	Cooper-Climax
20/11/60	Riverside	S. Moss	Lotus-Climax
08/10/61	Watkins Glen	I. Ireland	Lotus-Climax
07/10/62	Watkins Glen	J. Clark	Lotus-Climax
06/10/63	Watkins Glen	G. Hill	BRM
04/10/64	Watkins Glen	G. Hill	BRM
03/10/65	Watkins Glen	G. Hill	BRM
02/10/66	Watkins Glen	J. Clark	Lotus-BRM
01/10/67	Watkins Glen	J. Clark	Lotus-Ford
06/10/68	Watkins Glen	J. Stewart	Matra-Ford
05/10/69	Watkins Glen	J. Rindt	Lotus-Ford
04/10/70	Watkins Glen	E. Fittipaldi	Lotus-Ford
03/10/71	Watkins Glen	F. Cevert	Tyrrell-Ford
08/10/72	Watkins Glen	J. Stewart	Tyrrell-Ford
07/10/73	Watkins Glen	R. Peterson	Lotus-Ford
06/10/74	Watkins Glen	C. Reutemann	Brabham-Ford
05/10/75	Watkins Glen	N. Lauda	Ferrari
21/06/87	Detroit	A. Senna	Lotus-Honda
19/06/88	Detroit	A. Senna	McLaren-Honda
04/06/89	Phoenix	A. Prost	McLaren-Honda
11/03/90	Phoenix	A. Senna	McLaren-Honda
10/03/91	Phoenix	A. Senna	McLaren-Honda

UNITED STATES GRAND PRIX (EAST)

Races: 5   **First race:** 10/10/1976
Winner: James Hunt
Most wins (driver): James Hunt (2)
Most wins (constructor): McLaren (2), Ferrari (2)
Results 1976-1980

10/10/76	Watkins Glen	J. Hunt	McLaren-Ford
02/10/77	Watkins Glen	J. Hunt	McLaren-Ford
01/10/78	Watkins Glen	C. Reutemann	Ferrari

| 07/10/79 | Watkins Glen | G. Villeneuve | Ferrari |
| 05/10/80 | Watkins Glen | A. Jones | Williams-Ford |

UNITED STATES GRAND PRIX (WEST)

Races: 8   **First race:** 28/03/1976 - Long Beach
Winner: Clay Regazzoni
Most wins (driver): Clay Regazzoni (1), Mario Andretti (1),
Carlos Reutemann (1), Gilles Villeneuve (1), Nelson Piquet (1),
Alan Jones (1), Niki Lauda (1), John Watson (1)
Most wins (constructor): Ferrari (3), McLaren (2)

Results 1976–83

28/03/76	Long Beach	C. Regazzoni	Ferrari
03/04/77	Long Beach	M. Andretti	Lotus-Ford
02/04/78	Long Beach	C. Reutemann	Ferrari
08/04/79	Long Beach	G. Villeneuve	Ferrari
30/03/80	Long Beach	N. Piquet	Brabham-Ford
15/03/81	Long Beach	A. Jones	Williams-Ford
04/04/82	Long Beach	N. Lauda	McLaren-Ford
27/03/83	Long Beach	J. Watson	McLaren-Ford